Diana Dors

International Film Stars
Series Editor: Homer B. Pettey and R. Barton Palmer

This series is devoted to the artistic and commercial influence of performers who shaped major genres and movements in international film history. Books in the series:

- Reveal performative features that defined signature cinematic styles
- Demonstrate how the global market relied upon performers' generic contributions
- Analyse specific film productions as case studies that transformed cinema acting
- Construct models for redefining international star studies that emphasise materialist approaches
- Provide accounts of stars' influences in the international cinema marketplace

Titles available:

Close-Up: Great Cinematic Performances Volume 1: America
edited by Murray Pomerance and Kyle Stevens

Close-Up: Great Cinematic Performances Volume 2: International
edited by Murray Pomerance and Kyle Stevens

Chinese Stardom in Participatory Cyberculture
by Dorothy Wai Sim Lau

Geraldine Chaplin: The Gift of Film Performance
by Steven Rybin

Tyrone Power: Gender, Genre and Image in Classical Hollywood Cinema
by Gillian Kelly

Film Stardom in Southeast Asia
by Jonathan Driskell

Diana Dors: Film Star and Actor
by Martin Shingler

www.euppublishing.com/series/ifs

Diana Dors

Film Star and Actor

Martin Shingler

Edinburgh University Press

Edinburgh University Press is one of the leading university presses in the UK. We publish academic books and journals in our selected subject areas across the humanities and social sciences, combining cutting-edge scholarship with high editorial and production values to produce academic works of lasting importance. For more information visit our website: edinburghuniversitypress.com

© Martin Shingler, 2022, 2023

Edinburgh University Press Ltd
The Tun – Holyrood Road
12 (2f) Jackson's Entry
Edinburgh EH8 8PJ

First published in hardback by Edinburgh University Press 2022

Typeset in 12/14 Arno and Myriad by
IDSUK (Dataconnection) Ltd

A CIP record for this book is available from the British Library

ISBN 978 1 4744 7399 6 (hardback)
ISBN 978 1 4744 7400 9 (paperback)
ISBN 978 1 4744 7401 6 (webready PDF)
ISBN 978 1 4744 7402 3 (epub)

The right of Martin Shingler to be identified as author of this work has been asserted in accordance with the Copyright, Designs and Patents Act 1988 and the Copyright and Related Rights Regulations 2003 (SI No. 2498).

Contents

List of figures vi
Acknowledgements vii
Preface ix

Introduction 1

Part one: Stardom and celebrity
1 Bright (1946–9) 13
2 Blonde (1950–6) 31
3 Bold (July to November 1956) 51
4 Brazen (1956–85) 68

Part two: Acting and performance
5 Pseudo-star acting in *Is Your Honeymoon Really Necessary?* (1953) 89
6 A marriage of method and style in *The Unholy Wife* (1957) 99
7 Exploiting her nascent has-been status in *Berserk!* (1967) 109
8 Popping in and out as a virtuosic guest star in *The Pied Piper* (1972) 118
9 Perfect when poised in *Steaming* (1985) 128
Conclusion: A dubiously Dorsian conclusion 138

Bibliography 152
Filmography 156
Index 159

Figures

I.1 Screen shot from *It's Not Cricket* — 4
1.1 Screen shot of Dors with James Carney in *Dance Hall* — 28
2.1 Screen shot of Dors with Brenda De Banzie and Jack Buchanan in *As Long as They're Happy* — 44
3.1 Publicity still of Diana Dors in *The Unholy Wife* — 66
4.1 Screen shot of Dors with co-star Vittorio Gassman in *La Ragazza del Palio* — 72
5.1 Screen shot of Dors with co-stars Bonar Colleano and Sidney James in *Is Your Honeymoon Really Necessary?* — 97
6.1 Screen shot of Dors with co-star Rod Steiger in *The Unholy Wife* — 100
6.2 Screen shot of Dors with Tom Tryon in *The Unholy Wife* — 106
7.1 Screen shot of Dors with Ty Hardin in *Berserk!* — 116
8.1 Screen shot of Dors with John Hurt and Cathryn Harrison in *The Pied Piper* — 122
9.1 Screen shot of Dors in *Steaming* — 132
10.1 Cropped screen shot of Dors with John Moulder-Brown in *Deep End* — 140

Acknowledgements

First and foremost, I want to thank the editors Homer B. Petty and R. Barton Palmer for accepting this book for their *International Film Stars* series at Edinburgh University Press, as well as for their generous comments and support throughout the process. I would also like to express my gratitude to Gillian Leslie and her colleagues at EUP who have made the publication of this book such a painless, enjoyable and highly professional business. I'm particularly grateful to Sam Johnson, Eddie Clark and Caitlin Murphy, and freelance copy-editor Jill Laidlaw, for their skills, understanding, clarity, attention to detail and good humour throughout the production process. The research for this book has been conducted over several years and, consequently, many people have been instrumental in helping me, including numerous staff at the New York Public Library for the Performing Arts and at the BFI's Reuben Library.

Many leading researchers have inspired me: most notably, Richard Dyer, Christine Gledhill, Christine Geraghty, Pam Cook, Melanie Williams and Melanie Bell. I would like to thank Melanie Bell for allowing me to trawl through her personal archive and for the conversations we've had about Dors and other British female stars, as well as her unstinting support for this project. I'm particularly grateful to Giorgio Marina for identifying Rina Morelli as the Italian actress who dubbed Dors' voice in *La Ragazza del Palio*. While many of my friends have been encouraging and supportive, my thanks go especially to Ulrike Sieglohr for painstakingly reading through a full-length draft of the manuscript and having weekly conversations with me about the chapters as they evolved throughout lockdown. This significantly improved my study in addition to being enjoyable and highly motivating. As ever, I remain deeply indebted to my husband Simon Rushton, for his understanding, support and love, his proofreading skills and also for his delicious homemade flapjacks and scones. This book is dedicated to my friend Simon Millward, one of the most audaciously confident people I've ever met and a great giver of gifts that last a lifetime.

Preface

A spectacularly audacious and voluptuous forty-nine-year-old Diana Dors caught my attention when I was a shy and skinny fifteen-year-old. She first fascinated me in 1980 as the ball-breaking Commander wearing a camp military uniform in the television comedy series *The Two Ronnies*, simultaneously sexy and scary as the head of a matriarchal state police force, a supreme subjugator of men. The following year, I was mesmerised by her appearance as a glitzy fairy godmother in the pop music video for Adam and the Ants' hit single *Prince Charming*. Here, while Adam Ant repeatedly sang 'ridicule is nothing to be scared of', Dors waved her starry wand in the air and transformed his rags into 'glad-rags' so that he could attend the queerest of costume balls.

Now I can see why Diana Dors was so perfectly cast as Adam Ant's fairy godmother. For her role here is not simply to make his dreams come true but to inspire him to love himself and be proud. In so doing, this pop promo capitalised on Dors' reputation as a survivor despite disaster and derision, as someone who remained unashamed even when acknowledging personal failings and professional failures. Many people craved this kind of chutzpah in the early eighties. Her bravado was truly inspirational in an individualistic and highly competitive world. Yet I didn't know then that she'd been a major international sex symbol in the 1950s. Nor did I appreciate her skills as an actress, until I saw her some years later in *Yield to the Night* (Lee Thompson 1956). Watching this film, I marvelled at her transformation from a glamorous blonde salesgirl into a plain drab prisoner awaiting execution. Yet what was just as astonishing was the sheer intensity of her performance, notably in scenes with co-star Yvonne Mitchell as the caring guard with whom Dors' doomed Mary Hilton discovers a close bond of mutual understanding and sympathy, possibly even love.

It took several viewings of *Yield* for me to realise that this film is not a straightforward story of a young woman who loved a man so much that she committed murder to avenge his death. At some point it clicked and what I saw beyond this scenario was a much more tragic tale of someone who, in her bid to escape a loveless marriage, throws herself at a worthless man whose heart belongs to another. Even that's only half the story since, after signing her own death sentence by committing an act of premeditated murder in public, she meets a kindred spirit in the form of Yvonne Mitchell's Macfarlane. This prison officer not only confides in Dors' Mary but also comforts her on the eve of her execution and finally bids her an exquisitely painful farewell the next morning. The subtlety, sensitivity and subtext that Dors achieved when performing these scenes with Mitchell began to resonate forcefully with me over time. No wonder then that *Yield* has proven to be the single lasting testament to Dors' acting skills. It's an irrefutable fact that no other film exploited the precision, power and intelligence of her work as an actor to the same degree.

For years I failed to find anything to match this performance across the star's portfolio of sixty-seven films (see Filmography) and felt increasingly frustrated that producers hadn't provided her with any other vehicles worthy of her talent. It really did seem that *Yield* was the only film that showcased Dors' acting prowess, which is why I included a section on it in *Star Studies: A Critical Guide* (2012), noting how most audiences and critics in 1956 steadfastly refused to accept Dors as anything other than a frivolous sex symbol despite having proven her acting skills in a serious dramatic role (Shingler 2012: 131–3). When writing *Star Studies*, I discussed Dors in two chapters, one on publicity and another on the social and symbolic significance of film stars, never even considering using Dors as a case study in my chapter on acting. I regret that now.

It was after 2012 that I realised that Dors' other achievements as a film actor lay in fragments, small and often self-contained moments of a movie in which she performed a minor supporting or guest starring role. Consistently denied her own star vehicles and the opportunity to perform a main protagonist, Dors became an expert in creating star performances out of character parts, making her the mistress of the movie moment. She not only brought great skill and sound judgment to these small roles but also a vivid star image, a set of trademark gestures, an impressive amount of confidence and a great deal of poise, which meant that she never had to try too hard to gain audience attention.

I began to think about writing a book on Diana Dors after giving a series of presentations on her between 2012 and 2016, mostly at the *Celebrity Studies* conferences. These revealed a considerable amount of academic interest in this star beyond Britain, including Australia and the Netherlands. However, it was after reading Melanie Williams' *Females Stars of British Cinema* (2017) that I approached Edinburgh University Press with a proposal. EUP's International Film Star series seemed perfect for my study, giving Dors the chance to circulate more widely beyond British Cinema Studies while enabling me to indicate how she had been operating as an international movie star long before and after she went to Hollywood in 1956.

Working on this book over the last few years has given me the chance to really scrutinise and think about Dors' acting across the five decades of her supposedly undistinguished film career. During this time, I've gained a greater understanding and appreciation of the performer who caught my interest in 1980, someone who has impressed me ever since with her confidence, charisma, skills, intelligence, wit and resilience. My hope is that this book does justice to her talents and achievements as both a film star and actor, while inspiring others to delve more deeply into her extensive catalogue of films. For here remarkable things await discovery, even (or especially) in the very briefest of movie moments.

Introduction

Of all the celebrities that the Pop artists Jann Haworth and Peter Blake put on their Grammy Award-winning cover of The Beatles' album *Sgt. Pepper's Lonely Hearts Club Band* (1967), Diana Dors (1931–84) is the most eye-catching. Featured in the front row line-up, she stands out, resplendent in a gold figure-hugging shoulderless gown, threatening to steal the limelight from the 'fab four' at the centre of this crowded collage. Even the garishly coloured outfits of John Lennon (yellow), Ringo Starr (pink), Paul McCartney (blue) and George Harrison (red) are not enough to distract attention from Dors for long. There she stands with her hands on her hips, proud and poised, looking like the ultimate Hollywood movie star with her hair falling in large graceful curls to her shoulders, a stole hanging over her arms and evening gloves covering her hands and wrists. Presented in three-quarter profile, she gazes directly into the camera as a self-assured seductress. Who can possibly resist looking at her?

Dors outshines Mae West, Fred Astaire, Laurel and Hardy, Marlon Brando, Johnny Weissmuller and Marilyn Monroe in this luminous line-up. Not even Oscar Wilde, Karl Marx or George Bernard Shaw can distract from her for more than a moment or two. Haworth and Blake's placement of Britain's leading blonde bombshell here implies that if anyone could steal the show from the most famous group to ever come out of Liverpool – as well as their political, literary and pop culture idols – it was Swindon's Swingin' Diana Dors, known far and wide simply as 'Dors'. In 1967, The Beatles' latest chart-topping album secured her a prominent place in the pantheon of 20th-century icons, ensuring that the 32 million or so people that bought it would be sure to feast their eyes repeatedly upon her wax effigy – it was Diana Dors' twenty-five-year-old self that was moulded into wax and preserved as part of Haworth and Blake's photomontage. This meant that Dors' image remained in circulation on the cover of this celebrated record long after the Madame Tussauds Museum had melted down her dummy.

When the album was first released in May, Dors' film career had virtually collapsed, while her thirty-five-year-old face and body were accruing signs of middle-age. At a time when The Beatles enjoyed huge international success, Britain's former No. 1 Glamour Girl hit rock bottom as a public personality, being written off a 'has-been' (see Chapters 4 and 7). Although she had foreseen this some ten years earlier, even telling the American press in 1956 that she was planning to retire from filmmaking in five years' time (see Chapter 3), Dors carried on performing after her thirtieth birthday, seemingly unable to give up her place in the spotlight.

Seizing the spotlight

It was as a teenager in the late 1940s that Dors discovered that she could secure a place in the spotlight with the right hair, outfit, pose and glint in her eye (see Chapter 1). This is how, at the age of seventeen, she stole the show from under the noses of Basil Radford and Naunton Wayne when cast as a nameless blonde in their Gainsborough comedy vehicle *It's Not Cricket* (Rich and Roome 1949). From the moment her feet appear in a pair of stylish high-heeled shoes, Dors disrupts and captivates. As a glamour girl seeking a secretarial job at Radford and Wayne's private detective agency, she astonishes her potential employers with her full-lipped smile, luscious long-flowing shoulder-length light-brown hair and impertinent remarks.

Dors' nameless character – simply called 'Blonde' in the credits – might not really have blonde hair but she's certainly captivating. She's also 'forward' in the sense of being audacious and self-assured. It's her youthful charm that enables her to get away with such behaviour without causing any serious offence. The comedy of this scene derives largely from the way an unemployed working-class girl both enchants and disturbs two well-educated, middle-aged and middle-class men, robbing them of their patriarchal and class-based privileges, rendering them silly schoolboys.

Despite her youth, lack of education and lower social status, Dors' blonde character has a mature, knowing and sophisticated quality to her. Throughout this, her only scene in *It's Not Cricket*, she conveys a sense of being at ease, having a great deal of self-possession in the way she moves, speaks and looks at the men who are supposed to be interviewing her. She remains playful in her demeanour, conscious of being attractive without having to try too hard by preening, vamping or being overly sexual or smouldering. Seemingly easy-going, free-spirited and very natural in the way she behaves, Dors' character seems to take neither herself nor anything else too seriously. Nevertheless, there's something threatening about this sassy seventeen-year-old. Basil Radford's character is certainly unsettled by her.

When Dors looks directly into his famously scarred face, Radford laughs with embarrassment and finds it impossible to maintain eye contact. Taking advantage of his insecurity, she provocatively whips his tie out from his jacket with her finger while beaming at him suggestively and wiggling her shoulders. The embarrassed man averts his eyes when subjected to such saucy behaviour, avoiding to look either at the two strings of pearls around Dors' neck or at the plunging neckline of her pale ruffled blouse. Overcome by awkwardness, he stumbles in his bid to reply. The scene then becomes laughably Freudian when he toys with the end of his released tie. As the bold blonde continues to gaze into his averted eyes, he sneaks a quick peek at her cleavage, while Dors' beaming smile conveys a complete lack of shame on her character's part.

As Naunton Wayne says, hesitatingly, 'I suppose you realise that this job requires a certain ... experience', Diana slowly turns her head towards the right in the direction of his off-screen voice. She sways a little before turning round and walking towards him, the camera dutifully following. A pan to the right reveals the man standing nervously gazing at Diana as she approaches. His fiddling fingers emphasise his anxiety, provoked by a young woman who is not only bold and beautiful but also sexually assertive. Now giving Wayne a slightly impatient look, Dors says suggestively, 'That's my middle name, brother!' He laughs, pulling his head and shoulders back from her, indicating that he's taken aback by this brazen remark and by the idea that such a youngster should be so experienced. Diana is now strategically framed in the centre of a medium-long shot, with Radford on the left and Wayne on the right. She turns round to look at Radford as he begins to say, 'I feel that ...' and is interrupted by Wayne saying 'Oh, so do I', long before his colleague has made a coherent point.

Diana's question, 'When do we start?' elicits more incomplete and interrupted sentences from the two chaps, while Wayne possibly adds more phallic symbolism to this scenario of male inferiority when his hands reveal two pens in his waistcoat pocket (see Figure I.1). At this moment, Wayne prematurely interrupts his colleague's acutely

Figure I.1 Diana Dors as the 'Blonde', flanked by Basil Radford on the left and Naunton Wayne on the right, in a screen shot from *It's Not Cricket* (Rich and Roome 1949). (YouTube, last accessed 28/01/21.)

embarrassed comment, 'My partner and I feel that this post…' with the word, 'Exactly!', before adding, 'I don't think I could put it better myself.' When Diana asks in a small high and disappointed voice if they don't like her, Wayne insists that they do in an equally high voice, while Radford stammers the word 'absolutely' not only in high-pitched tones but also while emphatically shaking his head from side to side.

The scene reaches its comic climax when Radford begins his explanation with 'Don't get me wrong' and Diana shamelessly drops her gaze suggestively down his body until she reaches his crotch, smiling a little as she does so and swaying her shoulders gently. Having given him the 'once-over', she declares saucily, 'It would take a tougher dame than me to do that!' as she smiles and raises her eyes to look Radford squarely in the face. She pauses momentarily and rocks a little more before changing her tactics. Admitting defeat, she announces 'So long, boys!' with a smile indicating that she's not offended by their rejection of her. After subjecting Wayne to a lingering look, she departs from the shot. Yet Diana isn't quite done. For having walked to the door and opened it, she pauses and then turns back to face the camera. First, she looks intently and proudly in the direction of the two men. Then – and only then – she winks directly into the lens, laughs and turns around to exit the scene and the film.

Dors seizes the spotlight in *It's Not Cricket* by occupying what might be called the 'star slot' at the very epicentre of the screen. From here, she not only commands attention but also marginalises the film's stars. Their characters – Major Bright (Radford) and Captain Early (Wayne) – are not only side-lined but all too clearly intimated by her, fidgeting and tongue-tied for much of the scene. The actors themselves, meanwhile, compete with Dors for the audience's attention; such as when Radford plays with his tie and Wayne draws his head and shoulders back from Dors when addressed as 'brother'. As an actress in a bit-part with just one short scene and a few lines of dialogue, it would be expected that Diana Dors would overact to gain maximum attention. Nevertheless, she avoids the vivid facial expressivity and gestural over-playing commonly associated with character acting here (see Chapter 5). In fact, Dors performs her small nameless role as though she's the star of *It's Not Cricket*, seemingly confident in not having to work too hard to attract attention. When placed in the centre of the frame, Dors achieves this with ease.

Yet, while Dors doesn't over-play or over express to compete with the film's actual stars, she does gain a few extra seconds of screen time by dropping her gaze suggestively down Radford's body, assuming that an astute editor would retain this for its comedy value. She gains even more screen time when exiting the scene by pausing in the long shot that gives the audience a full-length look at her. The anticipated 'Take a last look, boys!' doesn't occur here, as there was presumably no such line in the screenplay. Instead, she audaciously winks directly into the camera, laughs and turns around before leaving. Such actions enabled Dors to stretch her scene out from under a minute to just over. Although this might not sound like much of an achievement, every second counts when an actor has only 1 minute in a movie.

A spectacular star and accomplished actress

Dors' achievements as a celebrity, photographic model, entertainer and actress were considerable, especially once she became a platinum blonde in 1951. The combination of a spectacular image, quick wit and considerable talent as a performer made her a force to be reckoned with. Consequently, she rose to international stardom as a curvaceous sex symbol in the mid-fifties (see Chapter 2) and, although her achievements as a movie star were cut short by scandal, age and weight gain (see Chapters 3 and 4), Dors not only remained a prominent public figure throughout her life but also endured as an iconic star long after her death in 1984 (see Marchant 2016: 261–76).

While photographs of her have proliferated on book and album covers, as well as across the Internet, Dors has become the subject of several biographies (see Wise 1998, Bret 2010, Prall 2018 and Cale 2021), a two-part mini-series on British television called 'The Blonde Bombshell' (Bierman 1999) and numerous academic studies, notably within the context of British Cinema Studies. It was just two years after the star's death that Christine Geraghty produced a short piece on Dors for Charles Barr's anthology of essays on British film history *All Our Yesterdays* (Geraghty 1986). This recognised the star as an iconic figure incarnating many ideological contradictions prevailing in British society and cinema of the 1950s. Dors' significance for British film scholarship was consolidated when Pam Cook published a chapter on her fifteen years later in Bruce Babington's edited collection *British Stars and Stardom* (Cook 2001). In these two accounts, Dors was acknowledged as one of the most important British movie stars of the fifties, while her stardom was attributed largely to her promotional skills, a specific appeal for working-class women and a propensity to embody emergent notions of femininity and sexuality in post-war Britain triggered by a consumer culture and an affluent economy.

It was Melanie Bell who highlighted the more international aspects of Dors' star persona when discussing *The Weak and the Wicked* (Lee Thompson 1954), *Yield to the Night* (Lee Thompson 1956) and *Passport to Shame* (Rakoff 1959). In *Femininity in the Frame* (2010), her revisionist history of women in popular fifties British cinema, Bell noted that Dors' highly sexualised image made her seem more foreign than British (2010: 146). This sense of foreign-ness or non-Britishness certainly marked Dors out as distinct from other native actresses working in popular British cinema at the end of the fifties, with her heavily sexualised persona being a key component of this. Yet this wasn't the only thing that made her seem more international as a star. A blatantly ambitious and self-promoting persona, a glitzy ersatz Hollywood image and much-touted dreams of Hollywood stardom also made Dors atypical as a female British film star (see Chapter 3). At the same time, the positive reception of her films in the USA from 1952 (see Chapter 2), along with her impact upon journalists and photographers at major film festivals in Venice and Cannes, respectively in 1955 and 1956, indicate that Dors was operating as an international movie star during this period.

The prominent place assigned to Dors in feminist film histories of post-war British cinema has ensured her legacy as a star while also conferring upon her a considerable degree of social significance. This makes her film work in Britain in the 1950s anything but negligible. Yet Dors' importance appears to lie chiefly in her stardom and celebrity (as an embodiment of British women's aspirations, dreams and desires) rather than in her accomplishments as a screen performer. In contrast, her versatility and flexibility as a screen performer have received relatively little recognition even though these were fundamental to her work as a film actor and crucial to her performances across a range of genres with very different kinds of directors and co-actors for no less than five decades. My aim here is to redress this imbalance.

About this book

Diana Dors: Film Star and Actor is a book in two halves. While Part One charts the rise and fall and rise again of Dors' film stardom across four separate chapters, Part Two analyses her performances in a selection of films from the 1950s to the 1980s. Chapters 1 to 4 explore the evolution of Dors' image through publicity and film roles, including her links with particular studios, publications and collaborators, as well as professional rivalries. Here, the emphasis remains largely on Dors as a public personality or celebrity. In contrast, Chapters 5 to 9 concentrate on her work as a film actor with close analysis of her acting in various cinematic genres, including British romantic comedy and Hollywood melodrama, children's fantasy and adult exploitation thrillers. This part of the book both highlights Dors' skills as a screen performer and raises the profile of some films that have so far received relatively little critical attention: namely, *Is Your Honeymoon Really Necessary?* (Elvey 1953), *The Unholy Wife* (Farrow 1957), *Berserk!* (O'Connolly 1967), *The Pied Piper* (Demy 1972) and *Steaming* (Losey 1985).

This book builds on and owes a substantial debt to a number of existing academic studies, such as Christine Geraghty's essay 'Diana Dors' in Charles Barr's seminal collection on British cinema *All Our Yesterdays* and Pam Cook's essay 'The Trouble with Sex: Diana Dors and the Blonde Bombshell Phenomenon' in Bruce Babington's *British Stars and Stardom* (see Geraghty 1986 and Cook 2001). Another key work is Melanie Williams' '"Blonde Glamour Machine": Diana Dors in the 1950s and Beyond,' the second chapter of her book *Female Stars of British Cinema: The Women in Question* (2017). By situating her alongside Glenda Jackson, Judi Dench and others, Williams recognises and celebrates Dors' acting skills. Yet, although this provides an incisive academic account of the star's career, it contains no actual analysis of her acting. It's partly this absence that motivated me to produce a book-length study of Diana Dors, one that explores her film work in terms of stardom *and* acting.

Melanie Williams' chapter cogently outlines the Diana Dors story, providing a succinct biography that extends from girlhood ambitions fuelled by Hollywood to her death from cancer in 1984. This includes the formation and disintegration of her sexy blonde bombshell image, her rivalry with Marilyn Monroe, the critically acclaimed *Yield to the Night*, the bad press and scandals during and after her Hollywood phase, before moving rapidly through bankruptcy, professional decline and expansion of her body to the actress's achievements on stage and television, culminating in her acquisition of icon status as a beloved British institution in the eighties. Williams' account of Dors' stardom contains many astute insights into the conflicting and contradictory aspects of her strengths and weaknesses, achievements and disappointments, highs and lows. Unfortunately, the brevity of this twenty-nine-page essay doesn't allow for an in-depth examination of the actor's performances in a range of films from across her thirty-nine-year career. In doing just that, my study is designed to augment Williams' chapter, embellishing rather than challenging it.

In the first chapter, for instance, I discuss Dors' acting in three very different films – *Oliver Twist* (Lean 1948), *Here Come the Huggetts* (Annakin 1948) and *Dance Hall* (Crichton 1950). The main focus is on how she acquired a distinctive screen persona as a 'Glamour Girl,' while adopting a number of trademark mannerisms. This includes a versatile acting technique comprised of posing, exuberant movement and the deployment of small naturalistic yet eye-catching actions. While this chapter discusses Dors' performances in a range of genres in the late forties, Chapter 2 focuses on her comedies during the early to mid-fifties. This includes how she gained a controversial reputation in America and Europe as a 'Bikini Baby'. It also discusses how the world's press began comparing her to Marilyn Monroe despite Dors' insistence on her difference by showcasing her sharp wit on stage, on screen and on the pages of some of Britain's most popular movie magazines.

Chapter 3 is largely concerned with the ambivalent and increasingly hostile press reaction to Dors in the USA during her short but career-defining spell at RKO. Dors' Hollywood debacle is charted here by examining the coverage she generated in leading American newspapers from the moment she arrived in New York at the end of June to her flight from LA in November, long before the release of her two Hollywood films, the crime melodrama *The Unholy Wife* (Farrow 1957) and the romantic comedy *I Married a Woman* (Kanter 1958). This chapter ends with a consideration of how Dors' image became tarnished after losing the much-hyped 'Battle of the Blondes' to Marilyn Monroe.

Chapter 4 begins with a discussion of the colourful widescreen romantic comedy *La Ragazza del palio* (Zampa 1957) that Dors made in Italy, considering how this was a perfect star vehicle for her. In stark contrast are her three British crime dramas of the late 1950s, referred to here as her 'Tart Trilogy'. Thereafter, having noted her brief second attempt at Hollywood stardom in the early sixties, I discuss Dors' return to Britain and the low point of her life and career leading up to her third marriage in 1969. This covers some of the minor roles she played during the sixties before exploring the revival of her film career in the early to mid-seventies, as well as how she regained kudos as an actor shortly before her death in 1984. As this chapter covers a long period in Dors' career, it adopts a snapshot approach, highlighting some key moments rather than providing a full review of all the films she made during her post-Hollywood years.

Part Two is comprised of shorter chapters that each analyse a film from different periods of Dors' career, starting with *Is Your Honeymoon Really Necessary?* (1953) in Chapter 5 and proceeding chronologically to *Steaming* (1985) in Chapter 9. This section focuses specifically on her acting and the ways in which she performed in romantic comedy (Chapter 5), melodrama (Chapter 6), exploitation horror (Chapter 7), children's fantasy films (Chapter 8) and feminist ensemble drama (Chapter 9). These chapters also introduce different ways of conceptualising screen performances, including pseudo-star acting (Chapter 5) and star-character acting (Chapter 7). Throughout Part Two, I repeatedly consider the differences between 'character acting' and 'star acting' but also such things as 'cameo', 'has-been' and 'ham' acting (Chapter 8).

It's in the second half of my book that I draw directly upon a number of major studies of screen performance. These include several essays that provide film scholars with useful ways of understanding different aspects of cinematic acting, including Barry King's 'Articulating Stardom' (1985), Ernest Mathijs' 'From Being to Acting: Performance in Cult Cinema' (2012), Paul McDonald's 'Story and Show: The Basic Contradiction of Film Star Acting' (2012) and Sarah Thomas' '"Marginal moments of spectacle": Character Actors, Cult Stardom and Hollywood Cinema' (2013). All of these are used in Part Two to help frame a discussion of Dors' acting, while shedding light on what actors do when they perform as stars but also when acting at different stages of their stardom – as rising stars, as major stars at their peak and as fading stars. Overall, the correlation of stardom and acting is the linchpin of my study of Diana Dors and, while stardom dominates Part One and acting is the focus of Part Two, these two components interweave their way through every chapter of the book. Consequently, at the very heart of *Diana Dors: Film Star and Actor* lies the interconnectivity of stardom and acting.

Part one
Stardom and celebrity

Chapter 1
Bright (1946–9)

Diana Dors appeared in an assortment of pictures during the late 1940s. Apart from one or two exceptions, the majority were pretty undistinguished and in most of them she was cast in small supporting roles with limited screen time and little scope for subtle or complex characterisation. She did, however, have the good fortune to work with some seasoned filmmakers such as George King, the director of her debut film *The Shop at Sly Corner* (1946), as well as rising new talents such as Ken Annakin, who directed her in *Holiday Camp* (1947) and *Here Come the Huggetts* (1948), among others. Nevertheless, her path to stardom was hampered by stiff competition from a multitude of talented, beautiful and revered actresses, who enjoyed great success in the post-war British film industry.

In his anthology *British Stars and Stardom*, editor Bruce Babington writes that the forties were 'a great period for British female stars', chief among them being Margaret Lockwood – the 'British Queen of Hearts' (2001: 95). Combining her 'nice ordinary girl' looks with a screen persona as a feisty and unconventional woman, Margaret Lockwood won the hearts of millions of British moviegoers, especially women, after her starring role in *The Wicked Lady* (Arliss 1945). If she occupied a place at the very pinnacle of British movie stardom at this time, Dors laboured away at the foothills. Having begun her film career at the age of fifteen in 1946, she became both an apprentice film actress at the Rank Organisation and a Charm School 'scholar' the following year.

When compared to Lockwood at this time, Dors' film career in the forties may well be regarded as negligible. However, as discussed in this chapter, her regular appearances in British films from 1946 to 1949 enabled the young actress to evolve a distinctive screen persona, one that deserves to be recognised as a significant achievement for a teenager attempting to break into a highly competitive industry.

As explained in more detail below, older actresses such as Jean Kent and Greta Gynt were the acclaimed bad girls of British cinema during this period and they were invariably first in line for starring roles as dangerous, loose and wicked women after Margaret Lockwood. It was partly Dors' youth that prevented a rapid elevation to stardom in the 1940s but her physical features also made her ascension to 'starlet' status something of a challenge. For instance, an adolescent pudginess lent her characters ample amounts of charm but this also meant that she didn't have the conventional facial features of most top female film stars; namely, large eyes, high cheekbones, straight noses, chiselled jawlines and long necks. Someone who did was Susan Shaw. Although now largely forgotten, she was one of Britain's most attractive and successful post-war starlets, one who consistently achieved larger roles and higher billing than Dors at Rank. However, it wasn't just Dors' face that hampered her rise to stardom but also her 'Glamour Girl' screen persona. This set her at odds with the times, which remained dominated by austerity, moderation, decorum and a puritanical ethos throughout the late forties.

Puritanical values characterised the Rank Organisation, despite the rampant sexual exploitation of young actresses by older males within various production departments. For Puritans like J. Arthur Rank, the owner of the Organisation, Dors' Glamour Girl image was only valuable as an object lesson in sin, as someone who either needed to be punished or redeemed at the end of a film. Many other prominent members of British society shared such a view, with senior politicians, civil servants, educators and members of the clergy considering glamour to be not only intrinsically shoddy but also inherently unpatriotic. While such attitudes prevailed in Britain, Dors' attainment of stardom remained highly improbable if not actually impossible.

This chapter explores Dors' film career prior to becoming a star or even a fully-fledged 'starlet,' concentrating in particular on how she perfected her screen acting skills and refined her onscreen image during this formative period. Scenes from various films are used to illustrate this, including *The Shop at Sly Corner*, *Oliver Twist* (1948), *Good-Time Girl* (1948) and *Here Come the Huggetts*. While many other examples could have been used for this purpose, these provide a representative sample of Dors' work at this time, indicating ways in which her distinctive screen identity first crystalised while laying the foundation for the glamorous persona upon which her stardom was eventually built.

Diana's roots (1936–48)

In her first autobiography, Diana Dors traced the roots of her acting career as far back as 1936 when her parents enrolled their five-year-old daughter in elocution classes in Swindon (Dors 1960: 5). Meanwhile, she traced her stardom back to a summer holiday in Weston-super-Mare when, at the age of thirteen, she came third in a beauty competition and had her picture published in a magazine (1960: 7). Shortly after this, she began earning money by modelling for US servicemen at art and photography classes, which led to her enrolment in one of Britain's leading acting courses at the London Academy of Music and Dramatic Art (LAMDA) in January 1946 (1960: 14). As a student, she won various awards for her acting and made contact with a casting director, which led to a screen test and an un-credited role in *The Shop at Sly Corner* (Cale, 2021: 16–17). This consisted of two short scenes in this screen adaptation of Edward Percy's play, devised as a star vehicle for Viennese actor Oscar Homolka.

Dors first appears 30 minutes into this film, fashionably and luxuriously dressed, looking every inch a model when leaning against a sports car. Despite being framed in a long shot, which displays her slender legs, Dors' trademark pout is clearly discernable here when her character demands a new pair of earrings from her upwardly mobile working-class boyfriend. Archie (Kenneth Griffith) is a calculating and rather fey young man whose principal source of income comes from blackmailing Desius Heiss (Homolka), an antique dealer and receiver of stolen goods. Having made a fleeting entrance as Archie's girlfriend Mildred in a scene lasting barely a minute, Dors re-appears a few minutes later, playing opposite Homolka himself. Here, she gets her first close-up as well as the opportunity to perform with the male lead for several minutes of screen time.

In terms of the early establishment of the Diana Dors persona, three things stand out about the actress's second scene in *The Shop at Sly Corner*. Firstly, she describes her love of glamour, makeup, fashionable clothes, luxury and glitz, including jewellery. This establishes her as a 'Glamour Girl'. Secondly, in a bid to maintain the older man's attention, she lifts her skirt to reveal her knees, signalling her awareness of her physical charms with the opposite sex and her determination to take advantage of this. Coy and flirtatious, her mood switches rapidly between a bored sulkiness and wild laughter. Finally, when Archie enters the room, he grabs her by the wrist and flings her out of the door, manhandling her and slapping her behind. 'Nice way to treat a lady', she declares as her parting shot, while stomping angrily out of the room. Despite her defiance, however, she complies with her boyfriend's wishes by leaving, albeit reluctantly and in a bad-temper. Mildred's treatment and compliance here suggest a certain degree of vulnerability, one that comes just moments after the display of her sexual power. Despite her ability to charm men, it's clear that she's also at the mercy of them. This quickly became a trope of many of the actress's films, as well as an enduring aspect of her star image and life story (Geraghty 1986: 343–4).

In these two brief moments from the actress's debut film, Diana Dors' glamorous star persona was born. She may have darker and more loosely flowing hair at this time but the factors that connect her appearance here with her subsequent star image include the sulky and provocative pout, the calculating glances, the richly resonant and highly modulated voice with a transatlantic lilt, as well as the posed and exposed luxuriously costumed body. In short, *The Shop at Sly Corner* presented Dors as sexually provocative Glamour Girl, one manipulated by working-class males. This constituted her 'type', which was subsequently recycled in different ways, giving her a recognisable – if stereotypical – screen persona that made casting easy for producers. Whenever a producer at Gainsborough Pictures, Ealing or Rank required someone to perform a small role as a Glamour Girl, Dors was invariably cast.

Having completed work on this film, the young actress swapped her father's surname (Fluck) for her grandmother's maiden name (Dors) and acquired Gordon Harbord as an agent. Harbord failed to get her the part of the Indian slave-girl Kanchi in Powell and Pressburger's *Black Narcissus*, which went to Jean Simmons (Wise 1998: 31). He did, however, secure her a day's work with Gainsborough Pictures dancing the jitterbug for a scene in *Holiday Camp* (Annakin 1947) starring Jack Warner and Kathleen Harrison as Joe and Ethel Huggett (Cale 2021: 18–20). Thereafter, Dors was cast in a small role in a Richard Attenborough crime drama called *Dancing with Crime* (Carstairs 1947). The part was too small to merit a screen credit. What it did do was bring her to the attention of producer Sydney Box, who not only cast her in a small named and credited role in *Good-Time Girl* (MacDonald 1948) but also helped her to secure a ten-year contract with the Rank Organisation with a starting weekly salary of £10 and annual increases designed to bring this up to £300 a week over the next decade (Wise 1998: 35).

Dors' time at Rank began auspiciously with a small role in one of her most prestigious pictures, an expensive expressionistic screen adaptation of *Oliver Twist*. This Cineguild production transformed one of Charles Dickens' best-loved novels into a work of art, complete with stunning lighting and set design, imaginative cinematography, authentic-looking costumes, hair and makeup, as well as fine performances from an array of talented actors. Produced by Ronald Neame and directed by David Lean, it starred Robert Newton as Bill Sikes and Alec Guinness as Fagin, with Kay Walsh as Nancy, Anthony Newley as the Artful Dodger and newcomer John Howard Davies in the title role. Dors, meanwhile, appeared as a minor member of the supporting cast, playing Charlotte, the disheveled buxom housemaid at Sowerberry's funeral parlour, where Oliver is recruited from the workhouse. She makes four brief appearances between the first 15 to 30 minutes of the film, having just three short lines of dialogue. Her first is, 'Oh please to come in, Sir' upon opening the front door of the funeral parlour to Mr Bumble (Francis L. Sullivan). Her second line is 'Yes, Ma'am' when Mrs Sowerberry (Kathleen Harrison) instructs her to feed Oliver, while her third line is 'He nearly killed the missus!' when describing the boy's frenzied attack.

With the exception of these three lines, Dors appears as a mute bystander and observer of Oliver's time at the undertakers. After introducing him to the place, she witnesses his first encounter with his nemesis Noah Claypole (Michael Dear). She plays a more active part in her third scene when she attempts to pull Oliver off Claypole during his assault and assists Mrs Sowerberry in carrying him across the room to confine him in a cupboard. In her fourth and final scene, she helps Mrs Sowerberry recover from her ordeal by flicking water over her and wafting her with a cloth. After this, she explains the nature of Oliver's misdemeanor to Mr Bumble and then observes Oliver's caning as the punishment inflicted by Mr Sowerberry (Gibb McLaughlin).

Diana Dors' most dramatic action in *Oliver Twist* is to scream when first seeing Oliver attacking Noah Claypole, while her most important act comes when helping Mrs Sowerberry restrain the boy. Otherwise, most of her screen time is spent observing the principal characters as they engage in dialogue, her gaze being transferred from one to another as they speak. Nevertheless, despite her incidental and largely silent role, Dors does command attention. In her second scene, for instance, she's shown standing at a kitchen table preparing vegetables for a meal. Here, while Oliver and Noah engage in conversation, Dors is framed in the centre of the shot and is well lit, revealing her shapely corseted figure as well as her grubby and disheveled appearance.

Similarly, Dors dominates the left-hand side of the screen during her fourth scene, being sufficiently well lit to reveal her reactions. What's particularly noticeable here is her open-mouthed shock on hearing that Oliver is not afraid. However, what can also be perceived is her approval of Mr Sowerberry's decision to punish Oliver with the cane and, finally, her ambivalent reaction to Mr Bumble's comment about his dead mother having shown great strength of character when she arrived at the workhouse on the point of giving birth. Although she has relatively little to do here, Dors occupies herself by rubbing her elbow, blinking her eyes and toying with the cloth in her hand, thereby attracting attention with these small naturalistic gestures. At the same time, her face conveys a mix of emotions, her condemnation of Oliver's violent outburst changing to admiration for his courage. Consequently, Dors' reactions help to emphasise the key point of the narrative, namely that Oliver's courage comes from defending his late mother from slurs to her character.

Dors' performance in *Oliver Twist* intimates that Charlotte has a greater level of perception than might ordinarily have been accorded an uneducated scullery maid. Though servile, she appears to respect Oliver for his rebelliousness. This ability to invest a bit-part with greater significance (or subtext) demonstrated that the actress was worthy of meatier roles. It would, however, be a long time before she was in a position to take on a leading female role such as Nancy, the quintessential 'tart with a heart'. Had Lean made this film after 1954, Dors might well have been cast in this role and could have excelled as a sexy, calculating and willful prostitute, one who is eventually beaten to death by her criminal thuggish lover Bill Sikes (Newton) when he discovers that she's betrayed him in order to save Oliver from a life of crime. In 1948, however, Dors was too young and too little known to take on such a plum role.

A bright future for a bright actress

When Diana Dors joined the Rank Organisation in 1947, her future seemed bright. Not only did she have a guaranteed income but also a contract with Britain's largest film company, one capable of competing directly with major Hollywood studios such as Metro-Goldwyn-Mayer, Paramount, Warner Bros. and Twentieth Century-Fox (Macnab 1993: 1). Rank owned many separate production companies, including Gainsborough, Ealing and Gaumont-British, making every kind of film, from fictional features to newsreels, live action and animated cartoons, adult and children's films, big-budget prestige pictures and programme fillers (or 'B Movies'). These were produced either at the massive studio complex at Pinewood or at other studios such as Denham, Lime Grove in Shepherd's Bush, and Islington. The films were then released widely across Britain and many other parts of the world by General Film Distributors, most being shown in over 600 British cinemas owned by the organisation, including the extensive Odeon circuit.

Through a series of acquisitions during the late 1930s and early 1940s, Rank secured the services of a large roster of star actors, including Margaret Lockward and Stewart Granger (Macnab 1993: 32). By the late 1940s, however, Rank was also in the business of grooming a new generation of movie stars along the lines of the Hollywood star machine. This included the 'Rank Charm School', which Geoffrey Macnab describes as a mixture of Lee Strasberg's Actors Studio in New York City and a London finishing school for young ladies (1993: 142). Set up under David Henley (a former general secretary of the actors' union Equity) at the Highbury Studios as a Contract Artists Department, this became known as the 'Company of Youth', where young contract players studied acting between film shoots (Wise 1998: 39).

While Olive Dodds was officially Henley's assistant, she was responsible for the day-to-day running of the Rank charm school, from selecting actors to refining their technique for the screen. As most of the 70–80 young contract players at Rank were drawn from repertory theatres, their stage acting skills needed modifying to be effective on screen with training in camera and microphone techniques. Dodds also supervised makeovers, which could involve dental procedures, hairstyle, makeup and fashion, as well as elocution and deportment (1993: 143). Despite all this, charm school 'scholars' were rarely selected for actual film roles since Rank's various production companies were not obliged to hire them (Macnab 1993: 143). Honor Blackman, Joan Collins, Diana Dors, Belinda Lee, Christopher Lee, Susan Shaw, Donald Sindon and Anthony Steel did better than most. The majority of actors and (most especially) actresses were sent out to make public appearances at garden fêtes and beauty pageants, as well as attending film and theatre premieres in towns and cities to generate publicity for the Rank Organisation. While most of her fellow scholars were 'headed towards oblivion', Dors was in the minority that secured film roles with companies such as Gainsborough and Ealing Studios (Macnab 1993: 140).

Dors joined Rank when the consortium revived 'B' feature production, churning out £20,000 movies at the Highbury Studios at the rate of one every five weeks (Macnab 1993: 146). This provided a valuable forcing ground for new talent, including actors and actresses. In 1948, Dors performed in films of variable quality, from the cheaply made murder mystery *Penny and the Pownall Case* (Hand) to the prestigious *Oliver Twist*. The former was a 'Quota Quickie', designed to meet the requirement that 45% of all films shown in Britain be domestic productions, as stipulated under 1948 Cinematograph Act (Cale 2021: 28–9). Rank and other British film companies went into overdrive to achieve this quota, leading to a multitude of minor movies. Rank starlets found it almost impossible to avoid these.

Rank starlets also found it hard to avoid predatory males. These young women not only had to contend with a culture of misogyny and sexism but also one that repeatedly exposed them to sexual advances by older male producers and directors unable to resist a pool of naïve, attractive and ambitious girls who were prepared to suffer all kinds of indignity in order to become rich and famous. According to Damon Wise, a physically advanced but sexually ignorant fifteen-year-old Diana Dors was forced to fend off a pass by the esteemed film director David Lean as well as an unnamed producer who instructed her to remove all her clothing when alone with him in a private room (Wise 1998: 47, 49). Rank starlets were clearly prone to sexual abuse and soon realised that a career in the film industry would entail the ever-present danger of sexual harassment and even rape. Developing the skills to deal with sexual predators might not have been part of the official charm school curriculum but it was certainly something that actresses needed to acquire when entering the film business.

Some sections of the Rank film empire, however, provided opportunities for talented women to prosper and occupy powerful positions, notably Gainsborough, headed by producer Sidney Box but run with his wife Muriel and his sister Betty. While Muriel took charge of the script department, Betty managed the Islington studios, where she oversaw the production of six pictures per year (Murphy 1989: 89–90). This included a series of low- to medium-budget social problem films, including *Good-Time Girl* starring Jean Kent as a working-class girl who ends up in prison as an accomplice to theft and murder after taking a job in a Soho nightclub. Despite it being a quick and relatively inexpensive production, this had an impressive cast that included Flora Robson, Dennis Price and Herbert Lom. It also contained some stunning noir-style cinematography and a Franz Waxman-style score performed by the London Symphony Orchestra. The screenplay was adapted from a novel by Arthur La Bern by Muriel and Sydney Box, with help from Ted Willis, and tells Gwen Rawling's story via a series of flashbacks initiated by Flora Robson's Miss Thorpe. The purpose of recounting this sad and sordid tale is to warn a wayward fifteen-year-old girl called Lyla Lawrence of the dangers of the London criminal and nightclub scene. Lyla, the girl in question, is played a sixteen-year-old Diana Dors, who appears sulking in the opening shots of the film when escorted up the stairs of the Juvenile Court to meet the magistrate Miss Thorpe.

Although Dors disappears for a long stretch of the film, she does reappear briefly halfway through as Miss Thorpe tells of how Gwen was brought before her in the court and sentenced to three years at an approved school. After another long flashback sequence recounting the rest of Gwen's unfortunate history, Dors finally returns for the conclusion. Her character Lyla has now discovered the terrible fate that awaits her should she pursue her desire for an independent life of glamour and excitement in London. Chastened and grateful, she exchanges her original sulky truculence for smiling gratitude while shaking hands with Miss Thorpe, revealing a sensible and pleasant side to her character before departing to return to her family home.

Although her appearances in *Good-Time Girl* are short and intermittent, Dors dominates the film in some ways, notably by coming at the start and the end. She may have very few lines of dialogue and minimal screen time, yet hers is a significant character because, as the recipient of Miss Thorpe's tale, she's placed in the position of the spectator watching the film, eliciting strong audience identification. Of course, with hindsight it's clear that Dors would have been a good choice for the leading role of Gwen Rawlings, had she been more established as a screen personality in 1948. Indeed, she could have played the sixteen-year-old tearaway to perfection, in contrast to the twenty-seven-year-old Jean Kent. Despite being too old for the part, Kent had an established reputation as Britain's 'Number One Bad Girl' and a fan club with over 20,000 members to help her draw large numbers of moviegoers to see *Good-Time Girl* when it was released into cinemas (Williams 2017: 37, 46). For as long as Kent retained a strong following, Diana Dors had very little chance of being cast in leading 'bad girl' roles at Rank and its associated studios. Her chances of gaining leading roles were also jeopardised by the Rank Organisation's prioritisation of the slightly older starlets Susan Shaw and Honor Blackman.

Battle of the charming starlets (1947–9)

As a Rank starlet between 1947 and 1949 (aged fifteen to seventeen), Diana Dors was put in direct competition with Susan Shaw, who was not only three years older than her but also lighter and prettier. Slender, with shoulder-length blonde hair and porcelain skin, Shaw had a classical beauty courtesy of perfect facial proportions and symmetry, a chiseled jawline, straight nose and large almond-shaped eyes. Hers was a beauty of almost glacial purity, suggesting dignity and refinement, one that gave her the potential to become a screen goddess. In 1946, she appeared as an extra in Sid Field's musical comedy *London Town* (Ruggles) before gaining a small credited role as Patsy Crawford in *Holiday Camp* (1947), the film that introduced Jack Warner and Kathleen Harrison's characters Joe and Ethel Huggett. In the second Huggett film, *Here Come the Huggetts* (1948), Shaw was recast as the couple's daughter Susan and played a more substantial role in the plot, although her part was larger still in the third instalment of the trilogy, *Vote for Huggett!* (1949). In 1949, Shaw was also cast as the female lead in *It's Not Cricket* (receiving third billing after Wayne and Radford), as well as co-starring with Derek Bond in the romantic comedy *Marry Me* (Fisher), for which she received second billing. This was all part of her strategic 'build-up' at Rank.

Susan Shaw's casting as one of three daughters in the Huggett films did much to make her a familiar face and name on British cinema screens in the late forties. Dors' casting as cousin Diana Hopkins in these films provided her with less screen time and dialogue than either Shaw or Petula Clark, who played the youngest daughter Pet. Nevertheless, Dors' Diana Hopkins certainly enabled the young actress to make a striking impression, most notably as a sexually mature relative who comes to stay at the Huggett home in *Here Come the Huggetts*, disturbing the family's moral order and daily routines. Diana is immediately set up as an over-developed bloodthirsty vamp, especially when shown gazing at herself in a full-length mirror in nothing more than her petticoat. She also raises her skirt above her knees whenever she sits down, just as she did in *The Shop at Sly Corner*.

Cousin Diana is sexy, seductive, bored and sulky but she's also smart in the sense of intelligent *and* stylish. She has a taste for the good life, consisting of fashionable clothes, dancehalls and nightclubs. She may not be the best-looking girl in town, since Susan Huggett (Susan Shaw) is noticeably prettier. However, Diana definitely makes the most of what she has. Hence, she's shown to be constantly maintaining her image by varnishing her nails, plucking her eyebrows and touching up her makeup. Her rather pudgy face consists mostly of her heavily painted luscious lips. Although her eyes are relatively small, her long dark eyelashes draw attention to them, making them highly expressive when it comes to conveying a range of ever-changing moods and attitudes, from 'come-hither' to 'get lost!' Thick glossy wavy light brown hair, falling just below her shoulders, frames this broad round face, with a parting on the left and a long snaking strand of hair falling down the right-hand side, often creating a 'peekaboo' affect across her right eye to make her just a little more tantalising in the style of the American star Veronica Lake.

While Cousin Diana is clearly attractive, enticing numerous male admirers within the film, she herself is drawn to tough guys with whom she dances energetically, again showing off her legs. When Dors dances, she does so with abandon, having an earthy and energetic quality to her movements. As well as dancing provocatively, her character also smokes and drinks. Being sassy, she's not afraid to cheek her superiors. So when approached by a policeman after being involved in a car crash, she's rude about his onion smelling breath, which results in her being arrested.

Playing Diana Hopkins in *Here Come the Huggetts* helped Diana Dors to fix her type and her star persona for British audiences. This role established her as a sexually advanced and rebellious good-time girl with a taste not only for glamour but also for tough, upwardly mobile men, men that invariably brought her into conflict with the law. These elements became familiar tropes in Dors' films of the 1950s as well as in her own life story, as recounted in her memoir *Dors by Diana* (1981). Consequently, this popular film franchise had a decisive impact on Dors' early film career, helping to transform her into a fully-fledged 'starlet'.

Edgar Morin, one of the first major theorists of stardom, defined the starlet as being 'halfway between the pinup and the star' (2005: 44). Writing in 1957 in his book *Les Stars* (which was translated into English by Richard Howard in 2005), this leading French sociologist argued that the starlet was 'originally almost-a-star, but in general today any young girl is called a starlet, even if she has never made a picture, provided she has an immense desire to be a star and gets herself photographed with a mention of her name' (Morin 2005: 44). Although Dors had appeared in eight films by the time she made *Here Come the Huggetts*, her starlet status was mainly established through regular appearances in movie magazines. In July 1949, for instance, a beautifully lit studio portrait of her appeared in Britain's leading film publication *Picturegoer* as part of a column called 'Looking at the Rushes' by Paul Holt. Underneath this image was the following statement: 'Diana at the crossroads. Her eyelashes and hips have got her so far. Now she must use her brains' (Holt 1949: 5).

Paul Holt's article was the first of a series designed to assess the merits of newcomers in 1949, a category to which Dors clearly still belonged after three years in the film business. In his assessment, the critic concluded that the young actress was 'walking a tightrope' and 'playing a very dangerous game' by 'playing off the men in the audience against the women' (1949: 5).

Holt warned Dors of the dangers of deliberately 'accentuating her most feminine attributes in order to interest men', stating that to succeed with this strategy she would need to 'use her brains'. If she became a 'full-blown vamp', he explained, she would have to be 'quietly sultry, not flamboyantly alluring' to avoid provoking laughter among her audience when playing her big scenes. Alternatively, she could 'do what Mae West did and make fun of the whole thing' but, he pointed out, this requires 'lots of wit, skill in delivery and a dream of a script writer' (5). Holt strongly advised the seventeen-year-old actress to think carefully about her progress, 'for there is no solid future in the type of parts she is being given now' (5). He also asserted that she had both the talent and intelligence to carry this off, stating that, 'Behind all those dropped eyelashes and swinging hips there is a sharp little brain and already enough training to pick up a laugh or even to pull a tear' (5). He ends his piece by stating that, 'this miniature Mae West may do very well indeed, if she does not allow them [producers] to push her around too much at this stage of her career' (5).

Written by a well-known film critic and former story adviser within the British film industry, this article was a warning to the young actress that she needed to use her own judgment when it came to making key decisions about her casting and the way she played her roles, being strategic about how she used her talent, training and intelligence if she was to become more than a Mae West impersonator and sustain a lasting film career. Whether or not Dors heeded Holt's advice to play down her sultry and flamboyant persona or to send it up, the actress did go on to do both, adopting a low-key acting style and a degree of ironic detachment from many of her characters (see Chapter 5). The significance of this *Picturegoer* piece in 1949 was that it established Dors as an actor with talent, skill and intelligence but also one with a recognisable acting style, involving a characteristic use of her eyelashes and hips.

Most stars have a style of their own, a distinctive way of talking, moving, standing, smiling and looking but they also have a clearly defined personality; in other words, a set of attributes and qualities (as well as opinions, attitudes and interests) that makes them interesting. These give them depth and detail as a person. Starlets, however, have often seemed too concerned with becoming stars and with acquiring the trappings of stardom (fame, wealth, luxury goods, etc.) to really have a personality of their own. In other words, their ambition for stardom seems so overwhelming that it leaves little room for them to acquire other interests, diminishing them as a person. As Morin wrote in 1957, 'The starlet is in search of the attributes of personality', adding that she does everything she can to fulfill the criteria for stardom in terms of how she looks, behaves, where she goes, how she dresses (2005: 44). Yet, for Morin, there remained a marked difference between the look and behaviour of stars and starlets. While the former avoid fans, photographers and crowds, the latter seek them out. While a star typically conceals her well-known identity in public behind a scarf or hat and sunglasses, the starlet tends to flaunt her body in public to attract attention, so that she 'takes her chances of becoming a star by means of the very photographs and attitudes that the star refuses' (Morin 2005: 44).

According to the definition of the 'starlet' that Morin proposed in *Les Stars* in 1957, Dors fell short of the starlet's exhibitionist, publicity-seeking behaviour in 1949, relying more heavily on her skills as a character actress to develop, enhance and refine her own unique screen persona as a Glamour Girl with a series of small roles. Dors' starlet status in the late forties came from being regarded as 'almost-a-star', although in the early 1950s (as explained in the next chapter) this evolved and brought her much closer to Morin's notion of the starlet as a young girl that 'has an immense desire to be a star and gets herself photographed with a mention of her name' at every opportunity (2005: 44). The problem for Dors in 1949 was that her 'almost-a-star' status was consistently undermined when the Rank Organisation promoted not only Susan Shaw but also Honor Blackman at her expense.

In 1949, after being reduced to a minor role in *Vote for Huggett!* (Annakin) and dropped altogether from *The Huggetts Abroad* (Annakin), Dors was cast in supporting roles in *A Boy, a Girl and a Bike* (Smart) and *Diamond City* (MacDonald). Both films enabled her to trade on and develop her naughty 'good-time girl' persona. However, these were both star vehicles for Honor Blackman, a sleek, chiselled-featured actress with more than a passing resemblance to Marlene Dietrich. Blackman, who began her film career with Rank in 1947 after graduating from the Guildhall School of Music and Drama, was cast in the leading female role in *A Boy, a Girl and a Bike,* playing working-class girl Susie Bates, who falls in love with the dashing and wealthy David Howarth (John McCallum) while on a group cycling trip in the Yorkshire Dales. Dors, meanwhile, was cast as the local good-time girl Ada Foster, who tries to lure Howarth away from Susie with her long legs, short cycling shorts and tightly fitting tops. Despite the fact that one of the characters in the film describes her as being 'built for pleasure,' Ada's all-too-obvious charms and no-holds-barred approach to seduction ultimately prove less effective at attracting the rich man of her dreams than the more demure and subtle attractions of her rival Susie Bates. However, despite the fact that her character's charms prove inadequate here, Dors did receive fourth billing for this role, which was a major promotion for her.

Dors was subsequently promoted to third billing in *Diamond City,* her name appearing directly under those of the two stars David Farrar and Honor Blackman. Here, Farrar plays Stafford Parker, a lawman in a diamond-prospecting town in South Africa, while Blackman plays Mary, a missionary's daughter (see Cale 2021: 38–40). In stark contrast, Dors is Dora, a barmaid and entertainer in a saloon, cutting a striking figure in her tightly corseted outfit, which accentuates her slim waist and burgeoning breasts. Her thick head of curly brown hair is mostly pinned up to expose her neck, which is adorned with either chokers or a tight string of pearls to make her appear older. Despite this, her broad face still looks very youthful, with an adolescent chubbiness that stands in stark contrast to Blackman's thin and angular features, conveniently highlighting their difference as women.

The rivalry of Mary and Dora for the attentions of Stafford Parker dominates and energises the film, culminating in an all-out cat-fight that has them rolling around on the floor tearing at each other's hair. Ultimately though, Dora turns out to be a 'good sort' when she retreats in order for Mary to claim the heart of the local lawman. However, in an unexpected twist of fate, Mary falls in love with someone else, conveniently leaving the coast clear for Dora to pair up with Parker after all. This proved to be one of the few occasions when Dors' character got her heart's desire at the end of the movie. Another rarity was that she not only got to dance but also sing in the film when Dora appears on stage with a group of attractive dancing girls to the delight of the crowded saloon packed with sex-starved prospectors.

Despite a strong performance in *Diamond City* in 1949, Dors subsequently failed to secure leading roles in Robert Donat's *The Cure for Love* (Donat 1949) and Jack Warner's *The Blue Lamp* (Dearden 1950), losing out to Dora Bryan and Peggy Evans respectively. Instead, she performed on stage in a string of productions, including John Willard's 1922 black comedy *The Cat and the Canary* (Dors 1960: 29). After receiving rave reviews for her theatre performances in Douglas Sargeant's musical comedy *Lisette*, Dors was promoted as the show's main attraction during its provincial tour in October 1949 (Bret 2010: 32). Thereafter, having showcased her talent as a stage performer, she returned to the big screen in a small role alongside Petula Clark in *Dance Hall* (Crichton 1950).

This Ealing film was produced by Michael Balcon and expertly directed by Charles Crichton shortly before he made *The Lavender Hill Mob* (1951). Although making little impression when released in June 1950, *Dance Hall* was exquisitely lit by Douglas Slocombe's team and imaginatively and tightly edited by Seth Holt. Art Director Norman Arnold designed stunning film noir-style sets for the unsettling and atmospheric nocturnal scenes. Meanwhile, the cramped domestic spaces in flats and small crowded working-class homes convey a strong sense of realism, anticipating the 'kitchen sink' dramas of the British New Wave movement of the late 1950s and early 1960s. The film also benefitted from some fine music and choreography, plus a spare and intelligent screenplay by Diana Morgan (with Alexander Mackendrick and E. V. H. Emment), one that skillfully blended drama and comedy, all of which made this one of the finest films of Dors' early career.

While *Dance Hall* starred Natasha Parry and Jane Hylton, with Donald Houston and Bonar Colleano as the male leads, Dors' role as factory worker Carole injected some much-needed comedy into an otherwise tense and somber film. Its overall tone is dark, being charged by the uncontrollable anger of Donald Houston's Phil, the frustrated desires of Natasha Parry's Eve, the mischievous philandering of Bonar Colleano's Alec and the quiet, patient suffering of Jane Hylton's lovelorn Mary. Dors only appears in a handful of scenes, although in each one she stands out, whether working at her lathe in the factory, dancing at the Chiswick Palais, chatting with her friends on the top deck of a bus, cheering on Petula Clark's character Georgie as she competes for a dance trophy or falling for a scruffy silent admirer (James Carney), who appears in Figure 1.1.

Dors' finest moment in *Dance Hall* comes when she climbs through the sash window of Georgie's home and chats with her parents, spinning around the room like a whirlwind. Throughout this and her other brief

Figure 1.1 A screen shot of the ever-mobile Dors sashaying towards her silent admirer (James Carney) in *Dance Hall* (Crichton 1950). (YouTube, last accessed 28/10/21.)

appearances, the eighteen-year-old Dors is vibrantly alive, exuberant, funny and charming, adding a light touch and infectious humour to each scene. Yet, in spite of her sterling work here, her contract with Rank was terminated at the end of 1949, shortly after the company announced net losses for the year and disclosed an overdraft of staggering proportions (Macnab 1993: 193). In an attempt to dominate the British film industry and compete with the major Hollywood studios, Britain's largest film consortium had massively over-extended itself during a period of economic instability. Consequently, drastic measures were required for Rank to regain a sound financial position as the 1940s came to an end. This included a reduction in its production roster, which was enabled by the Government changing the quota of domestic films in British cinemas from the original target of 45% to 30%. In addition to reducing production budgets, Rank closed its charm school and terminated the contracts of many of its staff.

Dors in the forties

Had the eighteen-year-old Diana Dors been in a reflective mood on New Year's Eve at the end of December 1949, she may well have been deservedly proud of her achievements during this tumultuous decade despite having failed to secure a single starring role. Since 1946, she had performed in fifteen films, no less than six being released across Britain in 1948 alone. In many of these she played a saucy Glamour Girl, which had quickly become her type. She played these, moreover, alongside some of the country's most popular stars, including Jack Warner, Petula Clark, Richard Attenborough, John McCallum and Anthony Newley, as well as some of the finest actors working in Britain during the postwar years; namely, Oskar Homolka, Flora Robson and David Farrar. She was also directed by some of Britain's best directors, notably David Lean and Charles Crichton, at leading studios such as Cineguild, Gainsborough and Ealing.

By working with these and other directors during this formative period, Dors evolved three distinct acting styles. The first was what might be called 'starlet acting', which consisted largely of provocative poses and pouts, using her eyelashes and legs to gain attention when having minimal dialogue. This involved certain postures – such as standing with her hands on her hips – to convey the attitude of her character. For this, she drew directly on her background in modelling, using many of the eye-catching techniques of the 'Pin-up Girl', along with facial expressions that could shift deftly between an alluring 'look at me' to a surly 'what are you looking at?' This style can be seen at work in films such as *The Shop at Sly Corner* and the Huggett movies.

The second style stood in marked contrast and involved a considerable degree of physical motion and kinetic energy, as displayed in films such as *Holiday Camp*, *Diamond City* and *Dance Hall*. Here, Dors conveys a youthful vitality and exuberance with abundant motion, notably (but not exclusively) when dancing, employing bold, free-flowing and apparently chaotic (yet presumably choreographed) movements. These derive from dance skills but also her lessons in deportment, which built core strength and stability, along with the ability to relax and control muscles, usefully conveying the vitality and suppleness of youth but also confidence and self-possession. With these two contrasting styles of performance, Dors brought a great deal of her own personality into her screen characterisations.

With her third acting style, however, Dors was able to better subsume her own personality into that of the character she was playing, such as Charlotte in *Oliver Twist*. Here, with a more theatrical mode of performance and costume, Dors used small gestures, expressions and looks to animate her character in the absence of dialogue in order to gain audience attention. She often performed small mundane tasks with her hands, adding naturalism to the scene, while facially registering reactions to her co-actors to suggest her concentration upon the key actions moment by moment. The latter often assists in drawing attention to the narrative significance of the unfolding events for the audience. This is where her drama school training, stage acting experience and her intelligence were brought into play.

These three distinctive acting styles drew directly upon different aspects of Dors' training and background – in modelling, dancing, deportment and stage performance – while making the most of some natural attributes. As a teenager, these gave her a comprehensive set of skills that established her as not only a consummate professional but also a conspicuously versatile performer. Although her rise to stardom was neither swift nor smooth (being hampered by competition from more classically attractive actresses such as Susan Shaw and Honor Blackman), it was certainly built on solid foundations.

Chapter 2

Blonde (1950–6)

Having performed in fifteen films from 1946 to the end of 1949, Diana Dors made another fifteen in Britain between 1950 and 1956. Once again, these comprised prestige productions with celebrated directors, such as Carol Reed's *A Kid for Two Farthings* (1955) and low-budget programme-fillers such as *My Wife's Lodger* (Elvey 1952). Apart from making a cameo appearance in *The Saint's Return* (Friedman 1953), she mostly received second or third billing during this phase of her career, indicating a significant rise in star status. Indeed, Dors transitioned from starlet to star when granted top billing for *Miss Tulip Stays the Night* (Arliss 1955) and *Yield to the Night* (Lee Thompson 1956).

Working mostly as a freelance actress during this period, Dors was employed by a range of studios, including London Films, Hammer and Rank. However, theatre remained an important outlet for the actress's talents in the early 1950s, particularly when film offers were scarce. In 1950, for instance, she received good press notices for her performance as Carmen in Kenneth Tynan's production of H. M. Tennent's play *Man of the World*, starring Roger Livesay at the Lyric Theatre in Hammersmith. After winning the *Theatre World's* 'Actress of the Year' Award for 1950, she was given the leading roles in stage productions of Peter Blackmore's *Miranda* and Garson Kanin's *Born Yesterday* (Bret 2010: 33–4). These plays consolidated her reputation as a talented actor while raising her public profile in Britain. Across the Atlantic, meanwhile, her films began to achieve good box-office returns in American movie theatres in 1952, notably when Launder and Gilliat's *Lady Godiva Rides Again* (1951) was retitled 'Bikini Baby' to highlight her role (as explained later in this chapter). It was largely her growing reputation in the States that persuaded Rank to re-hire Dors on a non-exclusive five-year contract in 1955.

During the early fifties, Dors transitioned from a leggy brunette into a busty blonde after bleaching her hair. As her breasts grew exponentially in 1953 and 1954, the actress found herself in much greater demand among British film producers, which resulted in her making more films in 1955 than at any time since 1948. This was an exciting time for Dors when she made a spectacular appearance at the 1955 Venice Film Festival in what was widely reported to be a mink bikini, as well as representing the British film industry at the Cannes Film Festival in 1956. Her off-screen exploits generated unprecedented levels of publicity and press interest for a British film star at this time, situating her in the world's press alongside leading international sex symbols such as Jayne Mansfield and Anita Ekberg (Cook 2001: 168). Meanwhile, her work on stage and screen continued to earn her awards and accolades, being voted Britain's top female film star in 1955 and winning the Variety Club of Great Britain's 'Showbusiness Personality of the Year' award in 1956. The combination of her film, stage and television appearances with her publicity stunts ensured that her celebrity spread widely to make her Britain's most notorious blonde, resulting in frequent comparisons in the press with Hollywood's hottest new movie star, Marilyn Monroe (Williams 2017: 68).

While the constant comparisons with Monroe infuriated Dors, the similarities and differences between these two stars and their careers proves instructive, hence the inclusion of a comparison in this chapter. Even at the risk of following such a well-trodden track, an examination of Diana and Marilyn's star images and working conditions remains significant for understanding both the success and failure of Britain's most famous blonde bombshell of the 1950s. Of course, the period under examination in this chapter is particularly well known and documented, having been discussed by several feminist film scholars, including Christine Geraghty, Sue Harper, Pam Cook, Melanie Bell and Melanie Williams (see Geraghty 1986, Harper 2000, Cook 2001, Bell 2010, Williams 2017). In fact, Dors' stardom in the 1950s has been so well documented by these and other academics that it's something of a challenge to shed any new light on this period, particularly as this invariably includes some of her best known films, notably her dramas *The Weak and the Wicked* (Lee Thompson 1954), *A Kid for Two Farthings* and *Yield to the Night*.

To avoid simply repeating the existing accounts, I focus below primarily on Dors' film comedies, in particular *Lady Godiva Rides Again*,

The Great Game (Elvey 1953) and *Value for Money* (Annakin 1955). While this makes for a more original discussion of this critical period in the star's career, it also reflects the fact that comedy became much more central to Dors' film work at this time, with nine of her fifteen films being comedies. Although it may seem odd not to include a detailed account of Dors' highly acclaimed performance in *Yield to the Night* here, this is precisely because so many existing studies of Dors' career focus on this particular film. Moreover, it's almost impossible for me to provide a more astute account of *Yield* than Steve Chibnall in his book *J. Lee Thompson* (Chibnall 2000: 70–103).

Britain's bikini blonde

When Diana Dors' film career all but collapsed in the early 1950s, she salvaged it by not only bleaching her hair and losing weight but also by becoming associated with a contentious little item of clothing called a bikini. A two-piece bathing outfit that covers beasts and pelvis but audaciously exposes the navel – therefore contravening the Hollywood Production Code of 1934 – the bikini was strictly for girls who dared to court controversy in the 1950s. Dors first sported a bikini on film in *Lady Godiva Rides Again* in 1951. She was then featured wearing one on posters for *The Last Page* (1952). In 1955, in addition to wearing a gold and black bikini in *Value for Money*, she was also photographed in a fur bikini by members of the international press as she floated down Venice's Grand Canal in a gondola.

For many people, the bikini was indecent. When French designers exhibited bikinis as part of their collections in 1946, several leading models refused to wear them. The Catholic Church in many parts of Europe was still denouncing them even by the late 1950s. The Miss World pageant banned contestants from wearing bikinis throughout the fifties despite the fact that this insidiously patriarchal annual event had begun life as a Bikini Contest at the Festival of Britain in 1951. However, after France's leading 'sex kitten' Brigitte Bardot adopted the bikini as part of her provocatively sexual image in 1953, many Hollywood stars were photographed in them, including Ava Gardner, Rita Hayworth, Lana Turner, Elizabeth Taylor and Marilyn Monroe. Diana Dors had beaten them all to it, however, being filmed and photographed in this immodest and contentious little garment two years earlier.

When Frank Launder and Sidney Gilliat cast the leading role of Marjorie Clark in a salutary comedy about the dangers of movie stardom for young attractive women, they rejected Diana Dors in favour of the unknown Pauline Stroud (Prall 2018: 43). Consequently, it's Stroud that plays a shopkeeper's daughter from the Midlands who comes first in the 'Miss Fascination' beauty pageant in Blackpool, winning a mink coat and a film contract, even though this sounds like the perfect starring role for Dors. After achieving instant celebrity by appearing on television, buses and billboards, Marjorie ends up performing semi-nude in a seedy revue, until her Australian boyfriend rescues her with a proposal of marriage in the penultimate scene of *Lady Godiva Rides Again*. When Australian masculinity is brought in to save the day, this film's retrogressive gender ideology becomes laughable. In overplaying its hand, this salutary warning to wayward aspirational women becomes the biggest joke of them all. Of course, like so many mainstream commercial films, *Lady Godiva Rides Again* plays it both ways, being sufficiently ambiguous to enable some viewers (women?) to interpret its repressive gender politics as laughable, while others (men?) can take comfort in its moral message as an example of good old common sense.

One of the true delights of *Godiva* is that it features a who's who of British film talent, with some of the country's most popular male movie stars like George Cole, Stanley Holloway, Dennis Price and John McCallum and an array of female talent, including Gladys Henshaw, Bernadette O'Farrell and Kay Kendall in supporting roles. There are also some delightful guest appearances from Googie Withers, Sid James, Dora Bryan, Alastair Sim, Joan Collins and Trevor Howard. So while the plot highlights the dangers of stardom for young women, the casting celebrates the achievements of many stars by including them in cameos, once more making this film's message regarding stardom ambivalent if not downright contradictory.

A major highlight of the film is Diana Dors as the experienced beauty queen contestant Dolores August. She makes a big impression despite being confined to a 20-minute section during the first half of the film and a brief re-appearance at the end. Dors is noticeably slimmer in both her face and physique than in *Dance Hall* (1950), and her luxuriant shoulder-length hair is distinctly lighter, although not quite fully blonde. Her new look is set off by an assortment of fashionable outfits, including skimpy lingerie. However, it's during the beauty parade that Dors really stands out as one of only two contestants to wear a bikini rather than a one-piece bathing costume. This is what the American publicists highlighted when selling the film in the USA, putting a bikini-clad Dors on the posters for *Bikini Baby*. As far as they were concerned, Dors was the star of this movie in spite of her limited screen time.

Dors' US reputation as a 'Bikini Baby' was consolidated in 1952 when she appeared in a two-piece bathing suit on the posters for *Man Bait* even though she never wears one in the film. In Britain, the same movie was released under the title of *The Last Page*. Directed by Terence Fisher for Hammer, this was a crime thriller based in a London bookshop, starring Hollywood veteran George Brent with Marguerite Chapman as his leading lady. Yet, despite receiving eighth billing in Britain for her role as the murdered sales assistant Ruby Bruce, Dors became the film's most notable figure when it was released in the United States.

Dors' chances of obtaining a Hollywood contract increased significantly when her *Bikini Baby* persona was publicised across the USA in 1952. After her marriage to the bit-part-film-actor-turned-salesman Dennis Hamilton in July 1951, he effectively took charge of her career and, in particular, her publicity by feeding stories to the press (Williams 2017: 62–3). One such story involved his wife turning down an offer of a Hollywood contract in order to go on making films in Britain (Dors 1960: 50). Hamilton was also instrumental in her doing product endorsements and advertising, as well as in propagating the myth of the glamorous Dors by associating her with expensive cars and luxury goods. After setting up Diana Dors Ltd in 1952, Hamilton masterminded a whole series of publicity stunts that positioned the actress as one of Britain's most exciting and extravagant stars (Dors 1960: 63). This image traded heavily on her established screen persona as a 'Glamour Girl' (as discussed in Chapter 1).

DD in David Dent Productions

Diana Dors (DD) became even more glamorous in 1952 after continuing to lose weight and bleaching her hair lighter still. Despite her increasing celebrity, however, British film producers were reluctant to offer her leading roles. The main exception was David Dent, who operated his own studio (Advance Films) as part of his family's business empire. This included Adelphi Films, a production and distribution company linked to Gainsborough Pictures. In 1952, Dent secured the services of veteran director Maurice Elvey, assigning him to direct three comedies featuring

Dors among the cast; namely, *My Wife's Lodger* in 1952 and *The Great Game* and *Is Your Honeymoon Really Necessary?* in 1953. None of these represented Elvey's best work or matched the quality of films such as *Bleak House* (1920), *The Hound of the Baskervilles* (1921), *Hindle Wakes* (1927), *School for Scandal* (1930), *Sally in Our Alley* (1931), *The Clairvoyant* (1935) and *The Lamp Still Burns* (1943). Indeed, Elvey's work for Dent was little more than serviceable. Yet, the director made increasing use of Dors' comic talents with each film.

All three Dent productions were based on stage plays. The first, *My Wife's Lodger*, was a star vehicle for the Northern music-hall comedian Dominic Roche. The second, *The Great Game*, based on a play by Basil Thomas, featured some wonderful characters, including a dodgy football club chairman, his long-suffering personal assistant and an apparently dippy but pushy junior secretary called Mavis Pink. Meanwhile, *Is Your Honeymoon Really Necessary?* was adapted from a stage farce by E.V. Tidmarsh, one that was filled with every cliché associated with the genre, including hiding under beds and in wardrobes, sleeping in bathtubs, throwing dishes and adopting aliases.

Dors got to dance a jitterbug, sing a sentimental number and wear a glamorous shoulderless evening gown and a pyjama top with no bottoms in *My Wife's Lodger*. For this, she received third billing. Nevertheless, this did little more for her than consolidate her type as an attractive and flirtatious Glamour Girl. In *The Great Game*, she performed as part of a fine ensemble led by James Hayter and Thora Hird, including John Laurie and Frank Pettingell. While Sheila Shand Gibbs played the not-so-ditzy-as-she-looked Mavis Pink, Dors was cast as fellow secretary Lulu Smith, a character with little plot significance. While adding glamour to an otherwise drab film, she did get to bodysurf over a real crowd of football fans at the Griffin Park ground during a match between Brentford and Blackpool Football Club, which was precisely the kind of stunt that in real life Dennis Hamilton was urging his wife to do in the early 1950s (Bret 2010: 36–86). The fine comedic performance skills that Dors had recently showcased on stage in *Miranda* and *Born Yesterday* were not required for this role. Instead, her role as Lulu Smith traded heavily on her newly acquired image as an ambitious publicity-hungry blonde bombshell prepared to do anything to gain public attention and media interest.

In *Is Your Honeymoon Really Necessary?* Dors was cast in one of two leading female roles as the successful glamour model Candy Markham.

As her name suggests, Candy is sweet, playful and charming, but she's no pushover. Indeed, she's sassy, sharp and fiery when crossed. In this role, Dors more than held her own with a consistently eye-catching performance that included the occasional wink to the audience and a low-key acting style that stood in marked contrast to the majority of the cast (see Chapter 5). Even though she wasn't *the* star here, she did receive second billing, while performing throughout with the insouciance of a major star in a minor movie.

DD v MM

In the early fifties, Diana Dors maintained her image as a Hollywood-style movie star by spending a large portion of her income on luxury goods and a fashionable wardrobe (Williams 2017: 62–5). Most of her earnings at this time came from stage work rather than filmmaking, even though by 1953 she was commanding fees of £1,000 to appear in such films as the Frank Randle comedy *It's a Grand Life* (Blakely 1953). Dors wrote in her first autobiography that,

> There was a brand new star being launched in America [in 1953] called Marilyn Monroe who was making films like *Gentlemen Prefer Blondes* and *How to Marry a Millionaire*, and the press, in their usual fashion, had retaliated with me as the British answer. . . . I had to live up to the new label and the publicity that went with it by competing with her films in such epics as *My Wife's Lodger* or this latest star-studded offer, *It's a Grand life!* (Dors 1960: 85–6)

Since the late 1940s, comparisons had often been made between Dors and Hollywood stars, including Mae West, Betty Grable and Lana Turner, but it was Marilyn Monroe (MM) that became her most cited Hollywood counterpart in the early to mid-fifties. This particular comparison is something that Dors continually resisted, as David Bret points out in his biography of the star (2010: 89–90). The comparison, however, is worth making.

Since December 1946, Twentieth Century-Fox, one of America's largest studios, had been grooming Norma Jeane Dougherty for stardom after recruiting this particular pin-up girl on a long-term option contract and changing her name to Marilyn Monroe. The actress had passed through the Hollywood star machine following a makeover that included the bleaching and restyling of her naturally brown and wavy hair, in addition to acting, deportment and elocution lessons. Walk-on roles in *Dangerous Years* (Pierson 1947) and *Scudda Hoo! Scudda Hay!* (Herbert 1948) led to small bit-parts with a few lines of dialogue in such films as the Marx Brothers' *Love Happy* (Miller 1949) and Bette Davis' *All About Eve* (Mankiewicz 1950). These launched her type as a 'dumb blonde', which was recycled in one film role after another.

Supporting roles in Jeffrey Lynn's *Home Town Story* (Pierson 1951) and Barbara Stanwyck's *Clash by Night* (Lang 1952) gave Monroe higher billing and even put her name onto the film posters, although under the movie's title. Such roles raised her public profile among moviegoers, while testing out the genres and types of roles she was best suited to. In 1952, Howard Hawks' comedy *Monkey Business*, starring Cary Grant and Ginger Rogers, provided compelling evidence that Monroe excelled in sexy dumb blonde roles and that large audiences could be drawn into cinemas when her name and image were featured prominently on posters, lobby cards and in theatrical trailers for a movie (Basinger 2007: 124–6).

Thereafter, Monroe received successive increases in salary as the options in her contract were taken up year after year. She was also given big-budget star vehicles, such as the crime thriller *Niagara* (Hathaway 1953), the musical comedy *Gentlemen Prefer Blondes* (Hawks 1953) and the western *River of No Return* (Preminger 1954). Being directed by some of Hollywood's leading talents, including Howard Hawks and Otto Preminger, helped Monroe to develop her acting skills and extend her range, particularly when assisted on set by acting coaches and dialogue directors. Other lessons about how to perform effectively for the screen were gained by playing opposite some of Hollywood's best actors and picking up tips from them or seeing how they worked. For Monroe, between 1950 and 1954, this included Bette Davis, Cary Grant, Charles Coburn, Joseph Cotton, Jane Russell and Robert Mitchum. Consequently, by the time she co-starred with Tom Ewell in Billy Wilder's highly acclaimed romantic comedy *The Seven Year Itch* (1955), Monroe's acting was deemed to be worthy of an award. For her role as 'The Girl' here she was nominated for the 'Best Foreign Actress' award by the British Academy of Film and Television (BAFTA).

By the mid-fifties, Monroe was not only one of the biggest stars in Hollywood and a famous figure across the world but also a consummate and idiosyncratic screen performer. Monroe had evolved a screen persona and set of mannerisms that were not only recognisable but also easy to imitate, notably the way she walked and talked but also how she used her eyes, face and body. While developing her screen acting skills in the early fifties, Monroe had also acquired her own unique brand of sexy blonde femininity, one that could be lucratively repackaged and sold to moviegoers around the world. However, Marilyn Monroe didn't become a huge movie star in the 1950s simply because one of Hollywood's largest studios built her up. It was, as Richard Dyer explains in *Heavenly Bodies*, because her image chimed with the times (1987: 19).

At a point in American history when the topic of sex was heavily debated, researched and contested, Monroe became the country's leading symbol of sex. She articulated prevalent notions of what feminine sexuality consisted of but also, and perhaps more importantly, of what type of woman American males judged to be the sexiest. Consequently, *Playboy* magazine declared Monroe to be the sexiest woman in the world (Dyer 1987: 27–40). Blonde, beautiful, buxom and curvaceous, she was constantly sexualised throughout her films and publicity, attention being consistently drawn to her body by movie cameramen, photographers, reporters and even film reviewers to the point where 'Monroe became virtually a household word for sex' (Dyer 1987: 23). The same, of course, could be said for Diana Dors.

By the end of 1954, twenty-eight-year-old Marilyn Monroe and twenty-three-year-old Diana Dors had made roughly the same number of films (25 and 24 respectively), having begun their film careers at virtually the same time after working as pin-up models (DD 1946, MM 1947). After becoming platinum blondes, they were both labelled 'blonde bombshells'. They were also called 'sex symbols' for the way in which they embodied an excessive and exaggerated femininity by using their curvaceous figures and luscious lips in a relentlessly flirtatious manner, maximising their physical desirability and sensuality (Cook 2001: 168–71). Everything about these women was calculated to enhance their sex appeal. They had, moreover, constructed for themselves a distinctive image that emphasised not only sexuality and glamour but also whiteness (Dyer 1987: 44–5). They could dance and sing as well as act, both performing regularly in dramatic roles as well as comedy. Yet one presented as dumb (MM) and the other as smart and 'sassy' (DD).

In his study of Marilyn Monroe and sexuality, Richard Dyer notes that there was a naturalness and innocence to her image, as well as high degree of vulnerability (1987: 32–6). He uses the terms 'child-like', 'emotional' and 'direct' to describe her (38). Part of her charm as the 'ultimate embodiment of the desirable woman' (42) is that she embodied male sexual desires in the 1950s while appearing to have none of her own. This made her purely the object of desire for the male characters in her movies and the men in the movie theatres. Had she possessed her own distinct sexual desires, these could easily have conflicted with the very ordinary male specimens on screen that typically become enchanted by her, such as Tom Ewell in *The Seven Year Itch*, not to mention those equally ordinary men that consumed images of her so avidly in films and magazines.

> Besides blondeness, Monroe also had, or seemed to have, several personality traits that together sum up female desirability in the fifties. She looks no trouble, she is vulnerable, and she appears to offer herself to the viewer, to be available. (Dyer 1987: 45)

It's here that we can see a parting of the ways between Marilyn Monroe and Diana Dors. Britain's leading Blonde Bombshell hardly fits the description of Monroe cited above. Indeed, Dors looked like trouble in most of her movies. It's true that there was a degree of vulnerability to Dors' star image (notably in the way that she was manipulated by her husband Dennis Hamilton) that occasionally surfaced or, more often, lay just below the surface of her screen roles (Geraghty 1986: 344). However, there was also a tougher aspect to her than Monroe, which manifested as a hard edge to her image in the fifties; notably, the rigidly lacquered hair, the enamel-like surface of her made-up face, as well as her tightly corseted costumes (Geraghty 1986: 345).

Dors seemed more 'put-together' (both constructed and artificial) than Monroe but also a lot more confident, self-possessed, commanding and demanding. These elements of her star image and screen persona threatened to undermine her role as the 'ultimate embodiment of the desirable woman' in Britain in the 1950s. In contrast to Monroe, Dors' cravings (sexual and otherwise) threatened to clash with those of her male admirers, while her strong sense of self-possession rendered her unobtainable. Her insistence on attaining her own desires made her more exclusive. How many of her male fans seriously thought she might give them a second glance? Dors seemed to demand attention and admiration in the fifties, whereas Monroe – very shrewdly – made her body available to be attained, objectified and desired without any strings attached. A higher degree of openness and naïvety made Monroe the ultimate sexual object.

Monroe's apparent naïvety was a major element of her 'dumb blonde' image, which seemed unquestioning, unthreatening, childlike, gullible, incorruptible, irrational and innocent (Dyer 1987: 36). Again, few of these elements pertain to Diana Dors in any straightforward way, even if at deeper levels some can be detected. Dors presented more explicitly as not only questioning but also challenging, as mature beyond her years, as calculating in addition to being hard to deceive, as clever and quick-witted (smart and sassy) and, in most of her iconic roles, as guilty of one crime or another (or, at least, one illicit desire or another), as discussed below.

The comparison with Monroe is instructive not only in terms of what made Dors unique as Britain's leading Blonde Bombshell of the 1950s but also of the ways in which her 'sex symbol' persona was always more threatening, radical and subversive than the label usually implies. For Dors' sex symbol image subverted many of the dominant notions of femininity that prevailed during the fifties, notions that associated femininity with such qualities as weakness, vulnerability, passivity, subservience and self-sacrifice. Yet there's a danger here in claiming that Dors' star image ran counter to prevailing ideals of femininity in Britain in the 1950s, as this risks oversimplifying a complex situation in which competing ideologies of sex, sexuality and gender circulated during this era across various different and distinct strata of an infamously class-bound society.

Melanie Bell has described the 1950s as a decade:

> ... lodged in popular consciousness as a period of gender conservativism, a time when women enthusiastically returned to their 'natural' roles as wives and mothers and readily gave up the employment opportunities and increased personal freedoms widely enjoyed during the Second World War. (2010: 1)

Although largely written off by generations of historians as a decade of domesticity for women and anxious conformity for all, Bell's *Femininity in the Frame* paints a different and more nuanced picture. It exposes the myth of the fifties as bland, conformist and inherently conservative, while teasing out the complexities and contradictions of gender in 1950s Britain so long hidden beneath the comfort blanket of 'history'. Her study draws out not just the many different types of working women in British films of the fifties but also the independent, non-normative and radical women that appeared in popular British cinema throughout this period. Here, Dors takes her place alongside many other notable stars of British cinema that presented progressive, ambiguous and contradictory forms of femininity, including Greta Gynt, Milly Vitale and Yvonne Mitchell.

In their own unique ways, Diana Dors and Marilyn Monroe were both shaped by and contributed to complex, contested and contradictory ideologies of sex, sexuality and gender circulating widely and forcefully throughout the 1950s. The major defining difference between them was that Britain's top blonde bombshell presented as smart (or sassy) while America's presented as dumb. For Dors, however, the most crucial difference was that Monroe had a powerful and prosperous studio behind her with a team of experts helping to produce her films and associated publicity. Dors, on the other hand, was largely on her own, after a short period under contract to the Rank Organisation (1947–9). Between 1951 and 1955, she mostly had a controlling and unstable husband trying to manage her personal and professional affairs. Unlike Monroe, Dors was also working in an unstable film industry that lacked the scale, profitability and standardised procedures of Hollywood to ensure a large and consistent output. While Monroe's rise to the highest echelons of Hollywood stardom between 1947 and 1955 was highly orchestrated, strategically managed and designed according to a set of well-established blueprints for success, Dors' progression was anything but progressive.

Like many British film stars, Diana Dors undertook theatre work and live shows when film roles were unavailable. Fortunately, she had the talent to be able to do this. She also had to be flexible in working for a range of different employers and crew. Three years at Rank and three films for David Dent's studio gave her some degree of continuity but nothing like that experienced by Monroe at Twentieth Century-Fox. Dors simply wasn't operating on an equal footing with her American counterpart. Recognising the very different industrial contexts in which these two actresses worked in the late forties and early to mid-fifties highlights Diana Dors' achievements within the British film industry. For Dors had accomplished a similar level of prominence in Britain as Monroe had in the United States despite all the obstacles in her way. Like Monroe, Dors had also managed to evolve her own glamorous persona, although one that in her case (and unlike Monroe's) was tough, intelligent and subversive.

The big year

1955 was a big year in Hollywood. Marilyn Monroe made an iconic appearance in *The Seven Year Itch*, her skirt billowing up to reveal her shapely legs, and spent time studying with Method acting guru Lee Strasberg at the Actor's Studio in New York. Marlon Brando, widely acclaimed as one of the finest exponents of Method acting, won an Oscar for his performance in Elia Kazan's *On the Waterfront* (1954). James Dean, also associated with the Method, not only made his cinematic debut in Kazan's *East of Eden* but also produced his iconic performance as the troubled teenager of Nicholas Ray's *Rebel Without a Cause* before dying tragically in a car crash. 1955 was also a big year for Diana Dors. Among other things, she received top billing for the first time, was re-hired by the Rank Organisation and achieved a major publicity coup with a spectacular appearance at the Venice Film Festival. Finally, and perhaps most importantly, she was voted Britain's Top Female Film Star. There's no doubt that Diana Dors had successfully transcended her starlet status to become a fully-fledged film star in 1955.

Five films featuring Diana Dors were released in 1955. These were *Miss Tulip Stays the Night*, also known as 'Dead by Morning' (Arliss 1955), *As Long as They're Happy* (Lee Thompson), *A Kid for Two Farthings*, *Value for Money* and *An Alligator Named Daisy* (Lee Thompson). Only the first of these was shot in black and white, and this was by far the cheapest, being produced by Bill Luckwell, a publicist-turned-film producer, who set up his own production company to make B Pictures. Despite receiving top billing for this, Dors was overshadowed by the scene-stealing antics of the veteran comedy duo Jack Hulbert and Cicely Courtneidge. Consequently, although Dors had a much smaller role in *As Long as They're Happy*, it more fully showcased her talents. Billed as a 'Guest Star', this colourful musical comedy gave the actress the chance not only to reveal a more buxom physique but also to sing and dance, as well as display her Diana Dors' star persona to the full.

Dors is thoroughly captivating in *As Long as They're Happy*, being vibrant and quintessentially herself in what was really a star vehicle for the Scottish-born entertainer Jack Buchanan, two years after he performed a leading role in Vincente Minnelli's MGM musical *The Band Wagon* (1953) alongside Fred Astaire and Cyd Charisse. Shot in Eastmancolor by Group Films Ltd (a Rank subsidiary), *As Long as They're Happy* was a lavish production aimed at the American market, one that boasted the best of British talent in minor roles. Despite considerable competition, Diana Dors made a big impression in her small role as an actress, singer and model named Pearl Delaney, appearing in just three scenes.

Dors makes an immediate impact when she first appears dressed in a skimpy pair of yellow shorts and an off-the-shoulder lime green top at the Hippodrome Theatre in London's West End. As she turns round to reveal her identity, she provocatively delivers her first line to David

Figure 2.1 A screen shot from *As Long as They're Happy* (Lee Thompson 1955) featuring a buxom Diana Dors as Marilyn Monroe-type showgirl Pearl Delaney being accused of being a 'brazen hussy' by Brenda De Banzie, while Jack Buchanan insists that she's a blonde. (YouTube, last accessed 10/2/2021.)

Hurst, 'Who do you think you are, Marlon Brando?' Her big moment comes at a party where she sings 'The Hokey-Pokey Polka' and flirts with Buchanan's character, ending up sitting on his knee in a shimmering sequined strapless pink evening gown that showcases the size and shape of her breasts, which are notably larger and more pointed than before.

While Dors' legs had featured prominently in the 1940s and her blonde hair had dominated in the early 1950s (in, for example, *The Great Game*), attention shifted to Dors' ample bosom in 1955. So, for instance, in her third and final scene, she appears in a black lace basque modelling for a painting by Buchanan. In this outfit, both her breasts and her slender legs dominate the scene, leading Brenda De Banzie (playing Buchanan's wife) to denounce her as a 'brazen hussy'. At this moment (as can be seen above in Figure 2.1), while De Banzie and Buchanan are strategically positioned in the foreground of the shot, Dors attracts the eye in the centre of the shot – what I'm calling the 'star slot' – with De Banzie's finger pointing directly to the guest star's left breast.

If Diana Dors used her small but showy role in *As Long as They're Happy* to advertise her assets to American audiences, a larger role in

Carol Reed's *A Kid for Two Farthings* gave her more kudos at home and abroad (Cale 2021: 70–2). This was a rare opportunity to work with an acclaimed director with an international reputation. After winning a BAFTA for *Odd Man Odd* (1947) and being Oscar-nominated for *The Fallen Idol* (1948) and *The Third Man* (1949), Reed's reputation was running high, his films associated with quality and prestige. It was a sign of distinction to be chosen for a leading role in a Carol Reed film in 1955, especially when cast opposite the revered actress Celia Johnson, who was the Oscar-nominated star of David Lean's 1945 romantic drama *Brief Encounter* and winner of the prestigious New York Film Critics Circle's 'Best Actress' Award. Being cast opposite Johnson in *A Kid for Two Farthings* made Dors a potential contender for a major film award herself. Unfortunately Reed's sympathetic, artful and intelligent direction didn't produce any awards or nominations for the principal members of the cast, although he was nominated for a Palme d'Or at the 1955 Cannes Film Festival for his joint role as Director and Co-Producer.

There was little expectation that Dors would win acting awards for her performances in *Value for Money* and *An Alligator Named Daisy*. Instead, they earned her far more money than any of her previous roles. After receiving £1,700 for *A Kid For Two Farthings*, Dors earned £5,000 for *Value* and £7,000 for *Alligator*, the latter being part of her new deal with Rank. Moreover, these romantic comedies had the potential to do well at the box-office in Britain and the USA. In *Value*, Dors plays an impecunious sexy showgirl called Ruthine West, while in *Alligator* she has a smaller role as Vanessa Colebroke, the daughter of a millionaire businessman played by James Robertson Justice. In the latter film, Dors looks more glamorous than ever in outfits designed by Julie Harris to give her the appearance of a Hollywood star like Lana Turner. Dors' stylish and spectacular look helped her to stand out among an extensive gallery of British talent that included Donald Sindon and Jeannie Carson in the leading roles, with Margaret Rutherford, Stanley Holloway, Ernest Thesiger, Jimmy Edwards, Patrick Cargill, Gilbert Harding, Frankie Howard, Nicholas Parsons, Joan Hickson and Stephen Boyd in small but showy parts.

Dors had a more substantial part in *Value for Money*, one that traded heavily on her own recent experience as a rising star of stage and screen, making her a perfect fit for the role of Ruthine. Performing opposite John Gregson and alongside Susan Stephen, Derek Farr, Frank Pettingell, Ernest Thesiger, Joan Hickson, Donald Pleasence and Leslie Phillips, Dors managed to dominate this movie from the moment she appeared on screen performing in a televised West End show called *Toys for Boys*. Later, in a short scene with Thesiger and Pettingell, she created a hilarious silent comedy skit involving the opening of a glass door, while elsewhere she sends herself up with a vampy dance number when auditioning for a show, only to be rejected on the grounds of having no figure.

Value for Money not only featured Dors in several song and dance numbers but also strongly resembled Marilyn Monroe's vehicles *Gentlemen Prefer Blondes* (1953) and *How to Marry a Millionaire* (1953) in which impecunious showgirls and models attempted to acquire rich husbands. In Ruthine's case this is Chayley Broadbent, the parsimonious heir to a Yorkshire rag factory who becomes besotted with her on a trip to London and invites her back to his home in the North as a special guest at the opening of a municipal playground. Here, Ruthine pretends to be a major star, which enables Dors to perform her blonde bombshell character with a high degree of self-mockery, exposing the heavily constructed and essentially performative nature of the glamorous sexy starlet. This is particularly notable in a scene in which she attempts – but fails – to seduce Chayley in a hotel suite wearing an off-the-shoulder pink negligee. In so doing, the film incited further comparisons with Marilyn Monroe, who not only frequently played performers in her films but also effectively performed femininity as a performance (see Solomon 2010: 111–14).

When released in the USA, *Value for Money* received a positive reaction. This may well have been due to the successful exploitation of Dors' talents as a singer, dancer and female impersonator. As far as one reviewer for the trade publication *Variety* was concerned, it was Dors that made this film worth the price of a ticket. Here, it was suggested that, while John Gregson's Yorkshire dialect might be an 'obstacle to extensive U.S. exhibition', the film benefitted significantly from 'a touch of spectacle in a couple of song and dance numbers.' It was, of course, Dors that provided the most notable touch of spectacle in these. Meanwhile, for the *New York Daily's* film critic Wanda Hale, it was Dors' outfits (particularly her bikini) that stole the show. 'Miss Dors is quite something to look at', Hale declared, before adding that one of the film's main attractions was 'Diana Dors in a parade of fashions, including a bikini that few showgirls could afford' (Hale 1957).

When the Rank Organisation re-hired Diana Dors in 1955, it was still Britain's biggest film company, profiting largely from distribution and exhibition. Between 1952 and 1955, Rank productions attracted large and lucrative audiences at home and overseas, although the North American market remained largely 'impenetrable' (Macnab 1993: 219). Diana Dors was re-hired as part of the company's renewed efforts to crack the US market due to the interest that American film distributors and audiences had shown in her since *Bikini Baby* and *Man Bait*. Dors' public profile in the States had grown significantly in 1955, particularly when she scored a major publicity coup in October with an article called 'Visible Export' in *Time*, one of the country's most influential magazines. This described her as the girl with 'the most libidinous lip in the business', declaring that, 'What Marilyn Monroe is to the U.S., what Gina Lollabrigida is to Italy, what Martine Carol is to France, shapely, blue-eyed Diana Dors, 24, is to Great Britain' (116).

The 'Visible Export' article in *Time* indicates several things about American attitudes to Diana Dors. Firstly, the statement quoted above situates her not only as Britain's sexiest movie star but also as one of the world's most beautiful women, as well as being Britain's version of Marilyn Monroe. In addition to highlighting her sexy lips, it describes Dors as 'a platinum blonde whose indefinable chemistry and heady allure have been greeted with international enthusiasm', reinforcing the idea of an international appeal based not only on her stylish image but also some less definable charisma that makes her interesting, intoxicating and captivating; the 'heady' quality here suggesting that she makes people's (implicitly male) heads swim.

In this article, Dors is presented as something for men to swoon over. It also indicates that the star had worked hard to become a highly paid vaudeville entertainer and film star, directly asserting that, 'Diana is tireless at publicizing Diana.' In Britain, such a comment would be implicitly critical but in America it's likely to have registered as a more positive attribute. After all, success in America (particularly Hollywood) required hard work and dedication, the ability to achieve high levels of income and to never shy away from self-promotion. Consequently, this article in *Time* suggested that Dors – more than any other British actress – had the appearance, appeal and attitude to make her a major movie star.

Baring all

After making *Alligator* for Rank, Diana Dors starred in the most important film of her career, an intense drama in black and white, one that delivered on the promise of her previous dramatic performance as a female prisoner in *The Weak and the Wicked* (see Bell 2010: 114–20). Produced by Ken Harper and directed by J. Lee Thompson for the Associated British Picture Corporation under the banner of Kenwood Productions, *Yield to the Night* (1956) stood in stark contrast to Dors' recent colourful comedies with musical numbers. This also marked a shift away from Hollywood-style confection to the kinds of British social problem films that had long dominated Dors' film portfolio, including *Good-Time Girl* and *Dance Hall*. *Yield* combined a crime thriller plot with psychological melodrama and social realism, employing these elements with subtlety and restraint, not qualities associated with the star by this time.

The combination of close shots (often from strange angles) with a spare *mise en scène* created an intensely psychological focus throughout *Yield to the Night*, one that fostered an emotional intensity among the cast rather than a dramatic expressivity. Bold and bare, this uncompromising film offered a highly credible, intimate and sympathetic portrait of an incarcerated woman awaiting execution. It also gave Dors far more screen time than ever before. There was no doubt that this was the perfect star vehicle for the actress in which she could display her glamorous image in the flashback scenes. Here, her character Mary Hilton is seen working at an upmarket cosmetics counter, falling in love with one of her male clients and becoming increasingly jealous of the other woman in his life. Meanwhile, the Dors' image was gradually stripped away in the prison scenes, the roots of her bleached hair showing, a lack of makeup revealing quite plain facial features, while her famous sex symbol figure was hidden beneath a shapeless prison uniform and nightgown. Without her usual star-defining accoutrements, the actress focused her performance on the intensely felt emotions of her character as her hopes of a repeal are dashed and the day of her execution relentlessly approaches. In the meantime, Mary forms close relationships with the women that guard her every hour of the day, particularly MacFarlane, played by Yvonne Mitchell. The growing bond between them adds a whole new dimension to what might otherwise have been a more straightforward salutary tale of a young woman whose untrammeled desires led her to commit a crime of passion over a feckless man (see Chibnall 2000: 93).

Diana Dors' star image and composure may have been stripped away in *Yield to the Night* but both were fully restored during the first months of 1956, particularly after she was voted Showbusiness Personality of the Year by the Variety Club of Great Britain in March (Bret 2010: 81). Shortly after this she was given her own regular column in *Picturegoer* called 'Out of Dors', providing her with the perfect opportunity to speak her mind about the state of her own movie career as well as commenting on the film industry in general. The headline for her column on 31 March ran, 'I'm going to speak my mind', beside an image of Dors in the shoulderless evening gown she wears in *As Long as They're Happy*. Above her head appeared the caption 'Britain's top glamour girl pulls no punches', although most of these were really bitchy sideswipes at her rivals, including fellow British blonde bombshell Belinda Lee, who Dors claimed was being constantly cast in her rejected roles (Dors March 1956: 8).

The headline for 'Out of Dors' on 14 April declared, 'I can't for ever be a glamour bombshell', under which she asks *Picturegoer* readers, 'How long can I go on with this glamorous bombshell nonsense?', before answering her own question with, 'Not much longer and I know it' (Dors April 1956: 8). Dors then explains that she took the part in *Yield to the Night* because, 'I had to show people I could act' (8). This was clearly her way of preparing her fans for the shock of seeing her de-glamorised in her next film but it was also a chance to indicate that she thought the whole glamorous bombshell thing was 'nonsense' and unlikely to last very long, thereby echoing Paul Holt's advice to her in the same magazine some seven years earlier, as noted in the previous chapter (Holt 1949: 5). In her April article, Dors also observed that someone like Marilyn Monroe could sustain a glamorous screen persona because she was given a succession of quality productions that were 'suited to her talents and ability' (8). This not only took a swipe at Monroe (and her limited acting skills) but also at Rank for not furnishing the British blonde with more star vehicles.

With a large readership of regular moviegoers, *Picturegoer* gave Dors the opportunity to establish a direct connection with her fans, while winning over her critics. Although the 'Out of Dors' columns typically featured images of her in sexy poses and glamorous outfits looking like a glitzy Hollywood movie star, Dors' statements emphasised that she was both fiercely proud to be British and a hard-working professional who took her craft as an actor seriously. It also revealed that she had strong views and was not afraid to articulate them. Yet this outspoken attitude didn't win her widespread favour among colleagues, critics and audiences. Indeed, a surfeit of Diana Dors' images and opinions throughout 1956 began to turn the tide of popularity against her just as she reached the peak of her stardom and was on the brink of achieving her long-held ambition of Hollywood stardom. Nine years of performing in small film roles had forced her to find ways of making maximum impact with minimal screen time. In 1956, however, with so many eyes now fixed squarely upon her, Dors was becoming over-exposed.

A blonde too bright and bold

Becoming a blonde certainly enhanced Dors' star profile in the early 1950s, maintaining her starlet status after Rank had dropped her. As a busty blonde, she had no difficulty in securing leading film roles in 1955, while attracting a considerable amount of public attention and press interest, enabling her to regain a contract with Rank on better terms. With her luminous locks and spectacular body, Dors finally achieved star billing in 1955 and a star vehicle the following year that fully exploited her image and acting skills. She also gained an outlet for her opinions in Britain's leading movie magazine in 1956. Growing recognition in the USA, Italy and France gave Dors an international reputation as one of Britain's most exciting and important film stars of the mid-fifties. This inevitably attracted interest from studio executives in Los Angeles, resulting in a contract with RKO in June 1956 that set the stage for the most dramatic episode of her career. This was her Hollywood debacle, which – although brief – proved to be Dors' defining moment, as explained in the following chapter.

Chapter 3

Bold (July to November 1956)

Diana Dors made two films in Hollywood for RKO during the second half of 1956. *I Married a Woman* was a romantic comedy starring George Gobel, which began shooting in July. In September, Dors replaced Shelley Winters as Rod Steiger's co-star in the crime melodrama *The Unholy Wife*. Both films received poor reviews and failed at the box-office when eventually released. In part, this was due to Dors' increasingly fraught relationship with the American press, although there are other reasons why these movies failed to impress critics and engage cinema audiences in the late 1950s, as discussed later in this chapter. The failure of Dors' Hollywood ambitions cast a long shadow over the rest of her career and had a pronounced impact on her star image. Nevertheless, as also discussed here, this failure actually reveals many of the star's greatest strengths, notably her courage, confidence and determination to be herself.

Impressing the press

Shortly before the release of *Yield to the Night* in London on 19 June 1956, Dors was offered £25,000 to appear in a Hollywood movie. By the time that Marilyn Monroe arrived in Britain to make what became *The Prince and the Showgirl* with Laurence Olivier at Pinewood Studios, Dors was making her way towards the USA on board the *Queen Elizabeth*. Arriving in New York City on 25 June, she held a press conference at the 21 Club alongside her husband Dennis, during which she informed reporters that her plan was to earn a fortune over the next five years and then retire to start a family (Wise 1998: 155). She described herself as being 'completely independent' and able to take on any kind of work anywhere in the world. When asked if she would be staying in Hollywood permanently, she replied emphatically, 'No. England is where my home is' (156).

Dors' made a deep impression upon several leading members of the New York press and inspired a great deal of newspaper copy over several weeks as journalists attempted to work her out. Here was someone who resembled Marilyn Monroe but didn't sound like her, someone who spoke with the confidence and authority of a leading statesman. According to her biographer Damon Wise, Dors became headline news with articles in all the major New York papers, including one entitled 'A Fascinating Fabrication of Femininity' in the *New York Mirror* and another headed 'Britain's Dynamite Explodes On The City' in the *New York Post* (Wise 1998: 157). On Monday 2 July, the *Post* printed another article on Dors, this time describing her arrival in Hollywood. It was entitled 'Men Don't Dare Look As Diana Comes Out,' which aptly conveys the sense of threat that Dors' fascinatingly fabricated femininity posed to many of the men she encountered at this time.

Of all the many newspaper articles that covered the story of Diana Dors' arrival in the USA there are two that stand out in terms of what they indicate about American press reaction to Britain's foremost blonde bombshell. The first was written by one of the country's most influential film critics Archer Winsten, being published in his regular movie column in the *New York Post* on 2 July. The second was by LA-based Hollywood journalist and writer Joe Hyams, who produced a syndicated film column in numerous publications across America. His article 'Sex with Wit', appeared in the *New York Herald Tribune* on 11 July, as well as many other papers. Together, these two pieces reveal an ambivalent reaction to the British actress that was a mixture of admiration and admonition, desire and disgust.

Archer Winsten's reaction to Dors was the most extreme of the two journalists. Having asserted that artifice was the keynote to her persona, he suggested that her femininity was fabricated, describing her 'most-improbable' hair colour and her 'eyelashes hung with black dew', as well as her 'dagger eyebrows'. The latter is a strikingly accurate description of the shape of Dors' dark eyebrows at this time but it also conveys a strong sense of menace by evoking the image of a sharp pointed weapon that can both pierce the heart and stab someone in the back. This apparently innocuous remark was undoubtedly intended to depict economically one of Dors' most unique and outstanding facial features. However, it simultaneously denotes a degree of danger, suggesting that there was something sharp and potentially deadly about Dors.

In addition to her dagger eyebrows, Winsten seems to have also been unsettled by Dors' 'hearty laughter'. The heartiness of her laughter implies that the twenty-four-year-old British actress managed to convey a great deal of self-assurance when meeting leading members of the American press on her very first day in their country, which seems remarkable given that this took place at one of Manhattan's most upmarket restaurants, the 21 Club being where the rich and famous went to see and be seen. Rather than being nervous or overwhelmed in such new and impressive surroundings, Dors displayed an absolute command of the situation with a relaxed demeanour that was made manifest through the way she laughed. There was clearly no trace of hesitancy or awkwardness on the part of this young British woman who had never been to the USA before. Her laughter seemed to emanate directly from her heart; that is, loudly, vigorously and with unqualified joy, ringing through the ears of the assembled illustrious company of mostly men.

Joe Hyams also noted the quality of Dors' laughter in his article 'Sex with Wit', having encountered her at her press conference in Los Angeles on 28 June. Hyams, however, described the Dors' laugh as 'lusty'. As with the term 'hearty', this conveys a strong and vigorous quality but with the addition of a more sexual connotation, the 'lust' part of the word evoking a strong sense of sexual desire – desire rather than desirability. Hyams also observed that, 'her eyes seemed to echo the joke long after the laugh ended', suggesting a knowing quality about this actress. He implied that Dors' was not only aware of the full implications of her various quips but also that she delighted in her audience's reaction to her witty remarks as they gradually realised the full implications of what she had said. This suggests that part of Dors' delight in cracking jokes came from being ahead of the crowd and waiting for everyone else to catch up with her.

One of the numerous similarities between Diana Dors and Marilyn Monroe noted by Hyams was that they were both 'adept at the quotable quote', regularly producing epigrams that captured the imagination and converted easily into newspaper straplines (Hyams 1956). Yet while Marilyn's bon mots typically seemed artless and innocent, Diana's came across as more calculated and knowing. The speed of her smart remarks was noted by Archer Winsten, who described Dors' 'quick answers' to the questions posed by the New York reporters, indicating that her intellectual reactions were as razor sharp as her dagger eyebrows. Yet what really fascinated him about Dors was the way she spoke. This prompted Winsten to make his most remarkable comment about her:

> Miss Dors stated, using a voice as British and authoritative as Winston Churchill's, that she had not considered most of her roles as acting. She was merely being herself. Speaking of herself, one could not avoid the thought that she had been pumped up, and that perhaps she would have to be taken out and reinflated in a few hours. (Winsten 1956)

There's clearly some suggestion here that the actress reminded Archer Winsten of an inflatable doll; in other words, a sex toy. When combined with the voice of the cigar-smoking and indomitable British wartime Prime Minister Winston Churchill, this creates an extraordinary combination of femininity and masculinity, as well as sexuality and power. While the inflatable doll inference possibly makes her more sordid than sexy, the Churchill reference connotes respect, authority and solidity, lending weight and bulk to what might otherwise be a slim and lightweight persona. The impression that Archer Winsten produced for his readers was of someone who might easily be deflated but never defeated.

What Joe Hyams found most fascinating about Britain's premier bombshell, on the other hand, was less her vocal tones and more the way she delivered her answers. In 'Sex with Wit', he noted that her 'answers to questions were direct and to the point.' This gave her a forthright quality, indicating someone who knew her own mind and spoke frankly. 'She appeared to laugh at herself', the reporter added, 'and her sense of humor never seemed obstructed by her own ego.' Hyams' seems to have been genuinely impressed by many of Dors' qualities and particularly those that made her seem different to Hollywood starlets, on the one hand, and other major British female stars, on the other. In terms of the latter, he described Dors as the 'antithesis of the traditional British female' since she was 'flamboyant, not dignified; obvious, rather than discreet; aggressive and not retiring; sexy, not sedate; ostentatious rather than modest' (Hyams 1956). This made her seem a far cry from such well-known stars as Vivian Leigh, Merle Oberon, Greer Garson, Deborah Kerr and Jean Simmons, who had all enjoyed success in the States by this time. These actresses had largely maintained a demure image when transitioning from British to Hollywood stardom, conforming to and confirming a widely held belief in the USA that British women were more reserved, restrained and understated than their American counterparts, as well as more introverted and sexually inhibited.

Rather than shattering American illusions about British femininity or presenting Dors as a new kind of Englishwoman in the mid-1950s, Hyams regarded her as an anomaly. This meant that the established national stereotypes of femininity didn't have to be rethought. While maintaining a neat opposition between American womanhood (as flamboyant, obvious, aggressive, sexy and ostentatious) and British womanhood (as dignified, discreet, retiring, sedate and modest), it also implied that Dors was – or wanted to be – more like an American dame than a British lady even if she did not want to become an American citizen and move permanently to the USA.

One of the things that struck Hyams about Dors and which made her seem different to many British stars was her skill as a self-publicist, the reporter recognising the adept way she handled members of the press, playfully engaging with them and giving them what they wanted, including good copy, an eye-catching quote for a headline or strapline and an alluring photographic image to accompany these. In his 'Sex with Wit' piece, Hyams reported that, 'Miss Dors frankly admitted she owes her screen personality to two things: sex and good publicity.' Elsewhere in his profile of the star, he depicts Dors as carefully crafting her public image in the way that she presents herself, quoting her as stating that, 'When I dress it's for men.' This established the star's presumption that she needed to maximise her appeal for male moviegoers if she was going to be a major movie star in the mid-1950s.

Dors' decision to enhance her 'male appeal' certainly made sense given that the gender balance of American cinemagoers had shifted to some extent from female to male since the late 1940s. This was partly in response to the 'Baby Boom' of 1948, which resulted in large numbers of American women staying at home to take care of their children, meaning that they watched television rather than going out regularly to the cinema as so many had done habitually before and during the Second World War. Of course, in order to attract the largest possible audiences to the cinema, Hollywood studios had never exclusively aimed films at females. Nevertheless, the content of many movies throughout the 1920s, 1930s and 1940s had been determined to a considerable degree by the studio executives' perceptions of female taste. Throughout this period, studio-era Hollywood also produced many films aimed squarely at female audiences with few concessions to what was perceived of as male taste, including Rudolph Valentino's star vehicles in the 1920s and Bette Davis' in the late 1930s and early 1940s.

By 1956, Hollywood studios were still making female-friendly films; notably, musicals, historical costume dramas, romantic dramas and romantic comedies. However, during the early to mid-fifties, many American moviemakers increasingly pandered to the needs, interests and desires of male cinemagoers. This was not only reflected in a preponderance of war films, action adventures, westerns, crime thrillers and fantasy films but also in melodramas such as *Written on the Wind* (Sirk 1956), starring Rock Hudson and Lauren Bacall, and comedies such as *Pardners* (Taurog 1956), starring Dean Martin and Jerry Lewis. Young adult male moviegoers were increasingly seen as a major contingent of the US film market, constituting a fairly coherent and identifiable group of dedicated filmgoers, especially at the 'Drive-ins'. This resulted in films such as *The Wild One* (Benedek 1953) starring Marlon Brando, *Rebel Without a Cause* (Ray 1956) starring James Dean and Natalie Wood, and *Somebody Up There Likes Me* (Wise 1956) starring Paul Newman and Pier Angeli. Therefore, while women remained crucial to the success of Hollywood cinema in the mid-fifties, the balance was shifting inexorably towards more male-centric movie fare, so that newly emergent female stars like Marilyn Monroe, Jayne Mansfield and Kim Novak were constructed and marketed largely (although not exclusively) in terms of their sexual appeal for (primarily straight) men.

Diana Dors' comments to Hyams, as reported in his 'Sex with Wit' article, suggest that she was aware that her star image was not only male-oriented but also overdone and excessive. For instance, she reportedly stated that, 'If I have to dress up I put on everything I own. Jewelry, furs, everything I can wear or carry.' This suggests that Dors believed that her target audience lacked subtlety and sophistication. Bearing in mind that many women in the 1950s prided themselves on their taste in clothes, hair, makeup and jewellery (since their social status depended largely on knowing about them), then Dors' deliberate flouting of the conventions of refinement or good taste implies that she staked her success on appealing to (straight) male rather than female sensibilities. Consequently, her spectacular image of glitter and tinsel was in all likelihood intended to maximise her appeal with heterosexual male moviegoers. A bold, unapologetic display of what many women (certainly middle-class women) and even many gay men might consider to be gaudy, tacky and over the top, was a shrewd and effective ploy to get herself noticed by male reporters and film producers, as well as the legion of male moviegoers that now constituted a very significant proportion of the cinema-going public in the USA and elsewhere.

Amidst all the eye-catching publicity-generating razzmatazz of Dors' press conferences in New York City and Los Angeles, there was also something frank, even rather brutally honest, about the way that the actress divulged her ambitions and her methods of achieving her goals. For instance, she informed the LA reporters that,

> I know that sex is a dangerous tightrope to walk but I figure if I'm lucky I can last for another five years. Then the public is going to want to know what else I can do. That's when I'd better have either talent or money in the bank. (Hyams 1956)

Perhaps the crucial thing to note about this is that Dors was not only being frank about her limited shelf life as a sex symbol in 1956 but also smart. She was undoubtedly telling the Hollywood reporters what they knew only too well. At the age of twenty-four, Dors clearly wanted it to be known that she was under no illusions about how far she could go in her career. At both New York and LA press conferences, she made a point of telling reporters that she believed that there could only be a few years of stardom ahead of her. Earlier, the New York-based film critic Judith Crist had reported in the *Herald Tribune* that Dors had declared that, 'About five years is the run of a star' (Crist 1956). Dors not only presented herself to the American press as knowing how to play the (publicity/ celebrity/stardom) game but also as knowing the unwritten rules of the film industry. She therefore impressed upon American reporters that she anticipated that her days as a sex symbol were numbered and that offers of leading roles in romantic comedies and dramas would decrease year by year after her thirtieth birthday. While this may seem to be a fatalistic and even defeatist attitude on her part, particularly when it's publicly announced on her arrival in the United States at the very start of her Hollywood career, it also implies a great deal of confidence. Dors was clearly establishing from the outset that she was no fool and this was part of a wider 'I'm not dumb' publicity campaign, which she used to distinguish herself from Marilyn Monroe.

Despite strenuous efforts to distance herself from Monroe, American reporters insisted on the likeness between these two blonde bombshells. Hyams, for instance, began his 'Sex with Wit' article with a description of Dors as 'the Marilyn Monroe of England', while disclosing her 'vital statistics – 36, 24, 36'. Here, he noted the 'striking physical resemblance between Dors and Monroe'.

> Miss Dors is amply proportioned; she always poses with her mouth slightly open because when it's closed she appears to be pouting;

> on important occasions she pours herself into vividly colored dresses designed to attract attention to her bosom overflow and wiggle-walk; she is completely unselfconscious. (Hyams 1956)

The revelation that Dors holds her mouth slightly open to avoid a sulky pout, that she pours her amply proportioned (apparently inflated) body into ostentatious outfits that showcase her large breasts by pushing them upward and outward (like balloons) and that she walks with a wiggle, makes her sound anything but unselfconscious in the sense of being ignorant of the impression she makes. Clearly, her image was calculated and constructed to ensure maximum impact (upon straight men). Here, the word 'unselfconscious' is used to assert that Dors was neither shy nor embarrassed about her extraordinary appearance.

Yet if Dors was not offended by such sexualised descriptions of her, she certainly grew increasingly impatient with the constant suggestions that she was like Marilyn Monroe and therefore made a more strenuous effort to distinguish herself. Consequently, three days after Joe Hyams' report was printed in the *Herald Tribune*, Dors' 'Out of Dors' page in *Picturegoer* included a major sideswipe at her American rival. After reporting how she had met various people since arriving in the States, including Julie Andrews and Elvis Presley, Dors described a conversation with the director Billy Wilder, claiming that he had told her 'that a certain blonde "hasn't yet made a good picture"' (Dors 14 July 1956: 11). Ensuring that readers understood which blonde Wilder was referring to here, Dors added that this was 'curious when you remember he directed her in *The Seven Year Itch*' (11). The British star had now thrown down the gauntlet, initiating a major battle between Britain and America's leading sex bombs.

The battle of the blonde bombshells

Judging by various reports in the American press, a public contest was waged during the summer of 1956 between Diana Dors and Marilyn Monroe, presumably to sell newspapers. For instance, William McCullam asked in the *New York American* on 5 August, 'Who is winning the Battle of the Bombshells?' Yet what's particularly interesting about this is the wartime spirit that it evoked, notably in the following questions, 'Is it Marilyn Monroe, who has invaded London? Or is it Diana Dors, her British counterpart, who has invaded Hollywood?' Clearly, such militaristic terminology was being used humorously. Yet the idea of Britain and America deploying a devastating blow to its rival film culture, not with long-range explosive missiles but rather the large torpedo-like breasts of Monroe and Dors, is both comical and intriguing. The terms and temperature of this debate suggest that there was more at stake in the image of a nation's sex symbol movie stars than simply ensuring big returns at the box-office by pandering to straight male sexual fantasies. These popular icons of female desirability appear to have assumed a high degree of importance within the complex realms of international culture, being dragged in to a conflict between two (once) close, proud and powerful nations. In other words, hyper-sexualised female stars played a role – at least in the imaginations of the press – in the post-war delineations of cultural power and status that emerged in the wake of the Second World War.

Monroe, as the better-known star in the USA, had less to gain out of this battle than Dors, who now had the chance to become as famous across America as her rival when this contest gained valuable space in leading US newspapers. Gossip columnist Louella Parsons, one of Hollywood's most influential women, played her part in sustaining this campaign on 26 August when she reported Dors as saying, 'I wish I could be called something other than England's Marilyn Monroe' (1956: 18). In an article entitled 'Diana Dors – Glamor from England', Parsons recorded Dors as saying that she wanted to be 'something more than just a fluffy blonde with visible assets' (18). Ironically, Parsons then recorded her measurements as 37" (bust), 24" (waist) and 35" (hips), giving her a slightly larger bust and slightly smaller hips than Joe Hyams did in his 'Sex with Wit' piece.

Louella Parsons' article appeared in the wake of a publicity disaster for Dors. At a gathering of Hollywood notables on 19 August, Diana and her husband fell fully clothed into a swimming pool and then physically attacked a press photographer after claiming to have been pushed into the water. News reports of this violent incident ran for days in the press, resulting in a headline in the scurrilous *National Enquirer* announcing 'Go Home, Diana – and take Mr Dors with you!' (Wise 1998: 176). The announcement that Dors was going to start shooting her second film for RKO in mid-August (a project entitled at this time 'The Lady and the Prowler') was overshadowed by reports denouncing the British couple for their bad behaviour and publicity-seeking stunts. Even in a land where self-publicists were generally respected as 'go-getters', they were deemed to have gone too far, resulting in a series of disgusted news articles. These shifted the balance in the Dors–Monroe battle decidedly in the American's favour.

Throughout September 1956, the hotly debated topic of Dors versus Monroe showed no sign of abating on either side of the USA. In New York on 24 September, Erskine Johnson announced in the *World Telegram* that, 'It's Swingin' Dors against Swivel Hips', in an article entitled 'Diana Competing for Marilyn's Role'. Despite clarifying that Dors didn't want 'to take over all of Marilyn Monroe's roles plus her title as Hollywood's No. 1 Sexpot', Johnson claimed that Dors 'is in the race for ... a couple of ... films intended for Marilyn' since Monroe went to England to make a film with Laurence Olivier. Six days later, on 30 September, British actress-turned-Hollywood reporter Sheila Graham confirmed in the *Sunday Mirror* that Dors 'resents' being called Britain's Marilyn Monroe (1956: 48). Sheila Graham's attitude towards her compatriot was less than friendly, the gossip-monger delighting in reporting that when Dors had reminded the film director Irving Rapper that they had met at Rank some years earlier, he couldn't recall the meeting. This disclosure rendered Dors eminently forgettable. By the time that *Yield to the Night* was released in the USA on 18 November 1956 under the title 'Blonde Sinner', Dors had fled the country leaving a trail of bad publicity behind her. The result was that the film failed to make an impact in the States. Meanwhile, having originally set a release date of January 1957 for *I Married A Woman*, RKO postponed it indefinitely fearing that Dors' reputation would damage the film's takings at the box-office.

A Hollywood dream becomes a nightmare

It's unlikely that *I Married A Woman* would ever have been a major box-office hit even if Dors had won the 'Battle of the Blonde Bombshells' and become the darling of the American press. Filmed in black and white with rather basic sets and props, this obviously low-budget production was clearly more of a B movie than a prestige production. It was certainly far removed from the likes of Marilyn Monroe's *The Seven Year Itch* (Wilder 1955) and Jayne Mansfield's *The Girl Can't Help It* (Tashlin 1956), both filmed in Cinemascope and DeLuxe Color at Twentieth Century-Fox. By the time that *I Married a Woman* was released in the USA, two years after being shot, the stakes were high in terms of competition in the romantic comedy genre. With its televisual aesthetic, low budget and poor script, it stood very little chance of being considered distinguished, innovative or original. Indeed, it was hardly a film at all.

I Married a Woman was George Gobel's second feature film and was designed to capitalise on his success in his NBC TV comedy series *The George Gobel Show*, which had been attracting high audience ratings since 1954. By 1956, Gobel's 'little man' persona (small in stature and status) had captured the public's imagination and heart. While his debut movie *The Birds and the Bees* (1956) was directed by Norman Taurog and written by Sidney Sheldon and Preston Sturges, his second was made by novice director Hal Kantor, who had previously been a writer on Gobel's television show, and was based on a screenplay by TV writer Goodman Ace, who was best known for his work on *The Milton Berle Show* from 1952 to 1954. Despite being shot by the experienced cinematographer Lucien Ballard, the camerawork was noticeably televisual, not just because of the black and white and narrow screen width but also due to a lack of camera movement, making it appear too static to really be a motion picture. Indeed, the film seems less like a B movie than a TV pilot and while *I Married a Woman* made for an inadequate movie it did have the makings of a successful TV sitcom, with various characters that could inject humour into one episode after another with multiple running gags, catchphrases and regular supporting characters: notably, Eddie, the Elevator Boy; Miss Anderson, the secretary with an ever-expanding vocabulary; Mrs Blake, the whining mother-in-law; and Bob, the playboy best friend.

Part of the problem with *I Married a Woman* was that its plot was little more than a series of comic episodes built around George Gobel's inadequacies as a husband, son-in-law, employee and friend. Despite having the odds stacked against him, Gobel's character Mickey duly becomes the family breadwinner, overcomes all the personal and professional problems that arise from having an attractive stay-at-home wife and an executive position, and becomes a father at the end. This scenario offered a comforting fantasy to small and largely insignificant men by insisting that even an inconsequential and diminutive man could still marry a smart, stylish and sexy woman like Diana Dors. While reassuring the small men of America, this small televisual movie was also something of an antidote to the big Hollywood epics starring America's biggest stars in the mid-fifties; Kirk Douglas, Charlton Heston and Burt Lancaster. While Dors might well have fared better opposite such stars, with her inflated physique and confidence, the actress found herself cast among the small fry and used to offer solace to the little folk with a preference for small screen entertainment over big screen dreams.

If *I Married a Woman* was designed to bring solace to little men, *The Unholy Wife* seemed designed to reassure America's larger than average males. In this film, a rotund Rod Steiger not only marries the most attractive (if dangerous and deceitful) woman in his life but also gains a son and heir. In a prison scene towards the end of the movie, his character Paul admits to his brother that his main motivation for marrying his wife Phyllis (Dors) was to be able to adopt her six-year old son Michael, after being informed by a doctor that he was unlikely to be able to father a child himself. In the closing shots of the film, Paul begins to educate the boy in the ways of wine growing, just as his father taught him and his grandfather taught Paul's father. The patriarchal line is now finally secure as Paul has a son that he can mould and train in the traditions of his family without interference from the child's mother, Phyllis, who has been conveniently executed for the murder of her mother-in-law. Consequently, this salutary tale not only offers a warning to men about evil wives but also offers hope to overweight and infertile men that they too can fulfill their patriarchal roles.

The ending of *The Unholy Wife* is wonderfully outlandish in the finest Hollywood traditions, especially those of melodrama. Dors' character Phyllis Hochen has almost committed the perfect murder and placed her innocent husband on death row. However, her evil plot is foiled when old mother Hochen (Beulah Bondi) takes an overdose of sleeping pills. As nobody believes the truth that she only gave the old woman one tablet (and was therefore not responsible for her death), Phyllis is convicted of murdering her mother-in-law, after which her lover San (Tom Tryon) testifies against her, helping to free her husband Paul from Death Row. With the exception of the priest, all the men in her life turn against Phyllis and support each other in order to reinstate the rule of moral and legal justice as enshrined under Christianity and patriarchy, even though it's the Hochen matriarch that has ultimately thwarted Phyllis' attempts to have her cake and eat it too.

On the point of inheriting the vast Hochen wine empire and having her rodeo-performing cowboy lover all to herself, Phyllis' intricately tangled web of murder and lies unravels. Yet, after hearing her confession, Father Stephen (her brother-in-law) forgives her for her sins against his family and exalts her to go to her death in peace. Finally free of the desires that have driven her to lie, cheat and destroy, Phyllis appears at the end of the film to have found not only peace but also salvation and is called to a greater love than sexual desire – in other words, to God. Delightfully incredible, this ending is balm for the souls of fearful men terrorised by cinematic femmes fatales for more than a decade.

There's another incredible Hollywood ending near the start of *I Married a Woman*. Mickey (Gobel) has taken his wife Janice (Dors) to the pictures to see a widescreen romantic drama starring John Wayne. Just before this movie ends, Wayne – the very embodiment of American masculinity – presents his wife (Angie Dickinson) with an expensive necklace for no other reason than that her loves her. It's like a nightmare for Mickey who appears to be the only man in the movie theatre. The women around him are entranced by this film's ridiculous happy ending. As well as succumbing to this fantastic spectacle, the women are also beguiled into a mesmeric state of wish fulfillment. Diana Dors sits beside him, wide-eyed, as though hypnotised by this widescreen colourful romance. When they leave the cinema, she remains lost in a dream world and appears to be walking on clouds as they make their way along the city pavements. Her head is now clearly filled with fantastical romantic notions of the perfect marriage and adoring husband. There's simply no way that little George Gobel's Mickey is ever going to match up to the strapping sensitive hero played by John Wayne on the screen, although at the end of *I Married a Woman* he does just that. At the same time, the real John Wayne, encountered on a cruise ship, is revealed to be a neglectful husband with a wandering eye for an attractive blonde like Diana Dors.

After a long career in Westerns and recent appearances as a washed-up pilot in William Wellman's *The High and Mighty* (1954), a merchant sea captain in Wellman's *Blood Alley* (1955) and the vengeful Civil War veteran Ethan Edwards in John Ford's *The Searchers* (1956), the very idea of John Wayne as a doting husband in a romantic drama seemed laughable in 1956. Likewise, a movie theatre mostly full of middle-aged women relishing the sight of John Wayne lavishing his wife with expensive gifts was just as big a joke in 1956 as Wayne being cast in such a movie. Yet the spectacle of the sassy British blonde bombshell Diana Dors being beguiled into believing such a hokey Hollywood 'Happy Ending' was perhaps the biggest joke of all. This multilayered gag not only pokes fun at the clichés of Hollywood romance but also the very idea that women might be susceptible to its charms and conceits. This early sequence from *I Married a Woman* is one of the few comic highlights of a film that proved hugely disappointing for everyone concerned with it, including the studio, its stars, the New York film critics and the minority of moviegoers that went to see it at the cinema in 1958.

RKO was collapsing by the time that work was completed on *The Unholy Wife*. At the start of November 1956, the press was baying for Dors' blood amidst reports of an extra-marital affair with her co-star Rod Steiger (Bret 2010: 112–13). Consequently, on 14 November, the actress made a quick exit and returned to London, leaving Universal Pictures to take on the distribution of *The Unholy Wife* in 1957 and *I Married a Woman* in 1958. Neither film made much of an impact upon release, being quietly consigned to the graveyard where most movies find a peaceful resting place after all the energy, excitement and frustration that went into their production.

The Unholy Wife was far less successful than Marilyn Monroe's crime thriller *Niagara* (Hathaway 1953), while *I Married a Woman* failed to achieve anything like the box-office returns, rave reviews or ballyhoo of Monroe's comedy *The Seven Year Itch* in 1955. Nevertheless, Dors' RKO movies reveal fascinating insights into the state of American masculinity in the mid to late 1950s. As the dream factory teetered precariously on the edge of disaster, maintaining a troubled relationship with television, these two movies suggest an attempt to offer male audiences comfort and reassurance; namely, that small men could become perfect husbands and large infertile men could become perfect fathers. However, these celluloid dreams are also suffused with nightmarish elements that threaten to undermine men and their traditional role as the head of the household. Spectacular blondes in the form of Diana Dors provide much more than a tantalising feast for male eyes here. These sexy sirens could, if unrestrained, destroy a man's world on account of them being desiring as well as desirable and smart rather than dumb.

An image both tarnished and enhanced by Hollywood

In an era when Marilyn Monroe prospered, Diana Dors failed, and did so spectacularly. The seeds of her failure to conquer Hollywood were sown the day she arrived and held a press conference at the exclusive 21 Club. Having already been associated with the indecent bikini several years before she arrived in the States, Dors' initial reception in New York and Los Angeles in June 1956 provoked an ambivalent reaction among leading American journalists and critics, many of whom were more disturbed than impressed by her image, voice and laughter, as well as by her frank and forthright comments. Condemnation grew as newspaper reporters and photographers became better acquainted with her, resulting in demands for her to leave the country. Leaving clearly wasn't easy, since it meant that Dors would forever after be associated with her failure to fulfill her much-touted Hollywood ambitions. Yet, by November, there was clearly no prospect of her staying put and trying to forge ahead in an industry so obviously set against her. If this wasn't the end of her campaign to take Hollywood by storm, it was certainly an inglorious retreat. Dors withdrew, deflated but undefeated.

Yet Dors didn't leave the USA empty handed. Not only had she been well remunerated for her RKO films but she had also received a Hollywood makeover that enhanced her already spectacular image, resulting in a series of glamorous photographs that would be used hereafter to record the moment when she was at the height of her international fame and beauty. The fact that Diana Dors looked exceptionally attractive in her two RKO movies resulted from work undertaken by a range of experts to perfect her image, notably a team of costume designers, makeup artistes and hair stylists led by Howard Shoup, Harry Maret Jr and Larry Germain.

Howard Shoup had a vast amount of experience by the time he designed Dors' costumes for her two RKO films in 1956, having worked with many of Hollywood's leading ladies since 1937. His long and impressive list of credits included designs for Joan Blondell in *The Perfect Specimen* (Curtiz 1937), Judy Garland in *Presenting Lily Mars* (Taurog 1942), Jane Wyman in *So Big* (Wise 1953) and Debbie Reynolds in *Bundle of Joy* (Taurog 1956). Hair stylist Larry Germain and makeup supervisor Harry Maret Jr also worked on the latter film and were no strangers to America's top female stars. Maret Jr, for instance, had done the makeup for Linda Darnell in the musical comedy *Everybody Does It* (Goulding 1949) and Jean Peters in *Apache* (Aldrich 1954), while Germain had styled the hair of Barbara Stanwyck and Marilyn Monroe in *Clash By Night* (Lang 1952) and Anita Ekberg in *Back from Eternity* (Farrow 1956). This meant that Dors' image was in very safe hands at RKO.

There's no doubt that the concerted efforts of Shoup, Maret Jr and Germain created a distinctive look for Diana Dors, as can be seen in the publicity photograph below, which was originally used to promote *The Unholy Wife*. Their efforts augmented her reputation as an attractive, fashionable and glamorous movie star and also helped her to stand out

Figure 3.1 Publicity still from *The Unholy Wife* (Farrow 1957). Creative Commons.

as one of the most spectacular features of her two RKO movies. When *The Unholy Wife* was released in the USA in October 1957, the *New York Herald Tribune*'s film critic Thomas Wood not only praised Dors for her 'brassy characterization' of Phyllis Hochen but also noted her stylish and 'revealing outfits that range from a form-fitting dress slit way up the back to a skin-tight, black turtleneck sweater and black toreador pants' (Wood 1957). Unlike Howard Shoup's costumes, there was little mention of the film's other aesthetic qualities or social significance.

Although *Variety*'s review for *I Married a Woman* in May 1958 announced in its headline that this old-fashioned George Gobel comedy 'doesn't come off' and was 'pretty tired stuff', it also noted that one of the few decent things about it were 'Howard Shoup's gowns for femme star'. For the picture, Shoup had designed a range of outfits to showcase Dors' physical assets, including a metallic pale blue swimsuit; a pale blue off-the-shoulder cocktail dress with golden rope straps and tightly fitted bodice, which was worn with a mink stole. He also created a deep red figure-hugging nightgown with lace bodice, thin shoulder straps and long split skirt designed to reveal the star's shapely left leg. Dors looked every inch a Hollywood movie star in these. Moreover, the outfits appeared in a range of publicity materials for the film, including numerous posters and lobby cards, as well as theatrical trailers.

While RKO's Technicolor film noir and black and white televisual rom-com failed to excite critics and audiences in 1957 and 1958, the styling of Diana Dors' image in Hollywood in 1956 certainly paid off. The work of Shoup, Maret Jr and Germain profoundly enhanced her Glamour Girl persona and made a lasting impact on her star image. Hereafter, a series of photographs preserved Dors' beauty and glamour for posterity, including the publicity photograph for *The Unholy Wife* featured above (see Figure 3.1). As she turned twenty-five, the actress realised her ambition of looking like a successful Hollywood movie star. This would, of course, make it even harder for her to maintain that glamorous image in the years that followed, these photographs marking the pinnacle from which she steadily descended.

Chapter 4

Brazen (1956–85)

> The whole town [Hollywood] was dead for me now. There were no plans for a new film. Socially I was no longer an interesting or even desirable person; just a blonde from Britain who made a bid for Monroe's title and lost the fight! There was only one thing to do, and dejectedly, on a grey November day, I flew home to England, vastly different from the star who had left in a blaze of glory months before. (Dors 1981: 167)

The way that she later recalled her departure from LA in her autobiography *Dors by Diana* suggests that the actress left in 1956 feeling deeply despondent. During that flight on 14 November, she had time to contemplate what the rest of her career might consist of now that her hopes of Hollywood stardom were dashed. She also had time to mull over how her five months in the USA had been transformed from the exhilarating high point of her career at the end of June to one of the lowest points in her life. Like so much about this ambitious and talented young woman, her fall from favour had been truly spectacular and, consequently, it was very hard to forget. Indeed, it would haunt her for the rest of her life.

Diana Dors' film career was no different to most other movie stars in that it consisted of highs and lows. Almost every major star experiences troughs in her or his career, however great or versatile. The onset of middle age often diminishes a glamorous female star's output, reducing offers of work and undermining her appeal for most moviegoers other than gay men. This makes forty a turning point in the working life of most leading actresses. The tragic deaths of Marilyn Monroe in 1962 and Jayne Mansfield in 1967 at the respective ages of 36 and 34 cut short their film careers but also spared them from the ravages of time and the indignities of being ageing sex symbols. Diana Dors' relative longevity, on the other hand, not only brought about the accretion of wrinkles and extra pounds of flesh but also made her a laughing stock as a grotesque blonde bombshell that had exploded in a most unfortunate way. There were two ways to deal with this, disappear entirely from the spotlight or remain in the limelight, sharing in the joke and laughing heartily at herself.

After choosing to go on working beyond her thirtieth birthday in 1961, Diana Dors struggled to secure movie roles. As her distinctive look epitomised fifties' fashion, she also had to contend with becoming an anachronism. Her corsets, basques, glistening pastel shoulderless evening gowns and mink stoles, even her big breasts and bouffant bleached hair, all belonged squarely to the 1950s. Increasingly, her saucy sexuality seemed too self-consciously poised and provocative in the 1960s, especially when set beside the raw and sheer matter-of-fact approach to nudity and sex of a rising star like Glenda Jackson (see Williams 2017: 118). Similarly, Dors' sex symbol persona seemed increasingly tame, fake and safe in the wake of films like *Saturday Night and Sunday Morning* (Reisz 1960), *A Kind of Loving* (Schlesinger 1962), *The Family Way* (John and Roy Boulting 1966), *Marat/Sade* (Brook 1967), *Up the Junction* (Collinson 1968) and *Women in Love* (Russell 1969).

Dors was never just about sex, however, as she also articulated female desire in terms of consumerism, incarnating the lavish excesses of Britain's 'Age of Affluence'. She personified the freedom to buy anything and everything but she also incarnated the increasing appeal of American goods, culture and lifestyle in Britain. During the sixties there was a seismic shift in which trade flowed across the Atlantic in the opposite direction when Americans increasingly desired, consumed and imported British goods; notably, fashion, pop music, art, literature and films. For a while, these were held to be cooler, groovier and much more trendy than their American counterparts. British things became desirable at home as well as abroad, resulting in a renewed pride in British styles, products and culture in the UK, including regional idioms and accents, as well as national idiosyncrasies. Britons bought British and capitalised on Britishness when selling and marketing products and cultural artefacts overseas. Dors fell out of step with the times in the sixties due in part to being an Americanised transnational star with an image steeped in old-style Hollywood glamour.

Yet if the times could change, so could Diana Dors. What couldn't be prevented were the tangible signs of her ageing body. Unlike many glamorous Hollywood stars (notably, Joan Crawford), Dors made few efforts to conceal these. Indeed, part of what makes her so special as a movie star is her insistence that the ageing and expanding female body be made visible and, furthermore, appreciated and enjoyed, even celebrated. The idea of hiding away as she aged and expanded was clearly an anathema to her. Dors steadfastly refused to be erased from public view or to feel shame for being older and larger.

Time, gravity and a healthy appetite changed Dors' image during the 1960s and 1970s. While her face noticeably hardened, her hair and body loosened up, softening and swelling. Casting off the corsets that pulled in her waist and thrust out her breasts, Dors could breathe better but also flow, giving her freedom and fluidity. Having given birth to three children, Dors' body took on many maternal aspects in the seventies (Williams 2017: 78). This was particularly noticeable in the increasing rotundity of her face and body but also her milky white long flowing hair, heavy breasts and her tired eyes. As a sensual maternal figure, she could be both arousing and threatening in her various guises. She could also be comforting and compassionate, seemingly both a source and recipient of unconditional love.

By the standards of Hollywood glamour, Britain's former No. 1 Glamour Girl and most famous blonde bombshell appeared to have 'let herself go' by the seventies. Nevertheless, by giving time, gravity and appetite almost free reign, Dors embodied prosperity and contentment, while acquiring a more unique and distinctive star image. She continued to revel in extravagance and excess as a big busty ageing blonde, insisting upon her desirability while declaring a taste for luxury and glamour without any concession to refinement, discernment or 'good taste'. The films that she made in the 1970s were mostly trashy, many being cheap and tasteless. Nevertheless, as I hope to show in this and subsequent chapters, Dors created some distinctive and distinguished film work after she was expelled from Hollywood in November 1956, enriching and diversifying her film portfolio with, if not great movies, then at least some great movie moments.

Winning and losing

While the public relations disaster that unfolded in the USA damaged her prospects in the American film industry in the latter part of 1956, this did not immediately impair Diana Dors' stardom in Britain and Europe, where she continued to gain leading roles and star billing. Indeed, the Italian producer Maleno Malenotti created the perfect star vehicle for her in 1957. This was a lavish widescreen romantic comedy in colour that showcased both the British star's beauty and the scenic highlights of Tuscany, notably in and around Siena and Pisa, while telling the story of how a young Texan woman called Diana Dixon (Dors) becomes the only female to participate in Siena's traditional bareback horserace around the Piazzo del Campo after winning a car, a wardrobe of clothes and sufficient funds to live like a princess in Italy for a week. By the end of *La Ragazza del Palio/The Girl of the Palio*, Dors' character has not only won these prizes in an American TV game show but also the horserace and the hand of a handsome, impoverished nobleman, Prince Piero di Montalcino, played by the good-looking and talented Vittorio Gassman, the award-winning male star of Giuseppe De Santis' *Riso Amaro/Bitter Rice* (1949).

La Ragazza del Palio was directed by the highly acclaimed and award-winning Luigi Zampa, who moved between Neo-Realist art films and more escapist commercial movies throughout the 1940s and 1950s, notably the Second World War drama *Anni Difficilli/Difficult Years* (1948) and the crime melodrama *Processo alla Città/ The City Stands Trial* (1952). *La Ragazza*'s score, meanwhile, was created by the award-winning Renzo Rossellini, widely celebrated for the music he created for the films of his older brother Roberto, notably *Roma città Aperta/ Rome, Open City* (1945), *Paisà/Paisan* (1946) and *Francesco, Giulare di Dio/Francis, God's Jester* (1950), as well as many other films, including *I fratelli Karamazoff/The Brothers Karamazov* (Giacomo Gentilomo 1947). Consequently, Gassman, Zampa and Rossellini ensured that *La Ragazza* was widely considered to be a quality production when it was released in Italy in December 1957.

In being colourful, playful, charming and finely crafted, this film was everything that RKO's *I Married a Woman* was not. Dors was given star billing here but, more importantly, she was also the central character, dominating the film from beginning to end even though her familiar vocal tones are entirely absent on account of being dubbed into Italian by a native speaker (Rina Morelli). In addition to looking beautiful and glamorous in a series of figure-hugging, eye-catching and stylish outfits, Dors' image was enhanced by playing a smart, self-possessed, pragmatic and progressive character.

Diana Dixon is in every way a winner and a woman who takes her success in her stride without it going to her head. When the playboy

Figure 4.1 A screen shot of Dors with Vittorio Gassman in one of her finest star vehicles, the lavish widescreen colour rom-com *La Ragazza del Palio* (Zampa 1958). (YouTube, last accessed 10/02/2021.)

prince attempts to seduce her, she deftly extracts herself from his love trap and teaches him a lesson into the bargain. When his haughty family treat her as a parvenu (labouring under the mistaken impression that she's a Texan oil heiress attempting to marry into the European nobility), she remains polite but unflappable, refusing to be patronised or manipulated (see Figure 4.1). Finally, after insisting on being allowed to ride the palio, to the shock and dismay of the all-male organising committee, she reveals her courage and equestrian skills. Indeed, throughout the film she insists on being accepted as an equal, whether as an American among Italians, as a commoner among aristocrats or as a woman among men.

The English writer Michael Pertwee (whose older brother Jon was a close friend of Dors) joined a large Italian scriptwriting team to help ensure that many aspects of the British star's persona were incorporated into the screenplay in order to make the role of Diana Dixon the perfect fit for Diana Dors. One such element was her own blue Cadillac, which gets stuck in the narrow backstreets of Siena. In many ways, the film became a showcase for Dors' personality and personal style, including many outfits that had previously featured in her publicity, such as a black halterneck top and a full-length shoulderless pink evening gown with a splayed fishtail skirt (as can be seen in Figure 4.1).

From start to finish, the Franco-Italian *La Ragazza del Palio* placed Dors at its very centre with everything designed to showcase her to best advantage, presenting her as a stylish and smart woman with modern attitudes, combining a respect for family life and national traditions with a defiance of restrictive gender conventions. She's also depicted positively as more of a 'role model' for liberated and independent women who wanted to do their own thing, breaking a few rules along the way and yet, like Cinderella, marrying her prince charming at the end. For once, she was no longer an object lesson in the form of an ambitious and highly sexualised young woman who needed to be either punished and/or redeemed.

Unfortunately, by the time this film was released in Italy (December 1957) and Britain (March 1958), it seemed that the world had fallen madly in love with a new blonde, one whose rise to stardom appeared to be truly meteoric after giving an erotically-charged performance in *Et Dieu ... créa la femme/And God Created Woman* (Vadim, 1956). After this highly controversial film was released in France in December 1956, 'Bardomania' seemed to spread like wildfire to make twenty-two-year-old Brigitte Bardot the newest, hottest and most popular sex symbol in the world. For a time, this attractive, charismatic and provocative young woman not only eclipsed Diana Dors but also mounted a very serious challenge to Marilyn Monroe's reputation as the perfect embodiment of desirable femininity.

Although it seemed to the world that this nascent and extremely nubile French star had sprung from nowhere in 1957, the truth was rather different. As Ginette Vincendeau observes in her book *Brigitte Bardot*, the young model-turned-actress and her husband Roger Vadim had been steadily orchestrating her rise to stardom since 1952 with a carefully choreographed campaign involving photographic modelling (largely for the magazine *Paris Match*), a succession of bit-parts in mostly comic movies and numerous eye-catching public appearances, notably at the Cannes Film Festival (2013: 7–34). Yet, as Vincendeau also writes, 'Bardot's fame grew exponentially in France after the release of *Et Dieu* in late 1956 and the first half of 1957' (2013: 38). Her global fame, meanwhile, came a little later following the film's 'spectacular American reception in October 1957', which involved breaking box-office records for foreign language movies in the USA (36).

By the end of 1957, Bardot had completely outstripped Dors in the stardom stakes and had done so without even setting foot in the United States (Vincendeau 2013: 38). She also became one of the world's biggest movie stars despite having been written off as a bad actor with a flat voice (25). Clearly what she lacked in acting talent, she made up for in terms of charm, style and sex appeal. Her long loose-flowing hair and the simple clothes that tightly hugged the contours of her long, slender and shapely physique gave her a type of 'anti-glamour' that set her apart from most other female movie stars in the fifties (17). Her youthful and unrestrained sexiness became a major part of Bardot's brand. Yet it was really only after bleaching her free-flowing tresses in 1956 and making a highly erotic appearance as Juliette in *Et Dieu* that she graduated from starlet to star, one whose name – even just her initials – rapidly became known to millions around the world.

As the embodiment of a free-spirited sexuality characterised by youth, agency and naturalism, 'BB' came to dominate the international spotlight in the late 1950s and subsequently maintained her dominance for most of the 1960s despite vehement public criticism. This made her one of the most contentious and admired stars on the planet, as much an icon and myth as a movie star (Vincendeau 2013: 53). During this same period, Dors was increasingly overshadowed and sidelined. Yet despite being trounced by both Monroe and Bardot in the popularity polls during the late fifties, Britain's most famous blonde bombshell clung on to the remnants of her stardom while continuing to carve out a distinctive film career over three more decades. Furthermore, she did so largely by exploiting her virtuosity and versatility as an actor just as much as her curvaceous figure and sex appeal.

The 'tart' trilogy

After returning from her aborted Hollywood career, Dors reclaimed her crown as Britain's No. 1 Glamour Girl with leading roles in *The Long Haul* (Hughes 1957), *Tread Softly Stranger* (Parry 1958) and *Passport to Shame* (Rakoff 1959). Injecting a heavy dose of sex and glamour into these films, she traded on her established glamorous persona, while proving that no one played a 'tart' quite like Dors. Although not considered distinguished movies at the time, they showcased her acting skills along with her shapely figure, while also revealing the different types of good-time girl that she was adept at creating: the good, the bad and the extraordinary.

The Long Haul was written and directed by Ken Hughes, most famous today as the director of the children's musical fantasy *Chitty Chitty Bang Bang* (1968). This Liverpool-born screenwriter and director carved out a niche for himself in Britain in the mid-to-late 1950s as a B-movie director working with imported Hollywood stars. *The Long Haul* was originally intended as a star vehicle for the American actor Robert Mitchum but was later adapted for his colleague Victor Mature. Dors, meanwhile, was cast as the lead female Lynn, the glamorous girlfriend of Joe Easy

(Patrick Allen), a crooked owner of a Glaswegian haulage company. She is, in essence, a 'tart with a heart', abused by her boyfriend and in need of protection, which is provided by Mature's Harry Miller, a tough but thoroughly decent bloke, the strong and silent type.

After supporting Mature in *The Long Haul* and starring in *La Ragazza del Palio*, Dors was given top billing for her next two movies *Tread Softly Stranger* and *Passport to Shame*, which were released in Britain in 1958 and 1959 respectively. In both cases, her fame put her name above the title, giving her star billing for what were really supporting roles. In the first of these, she plays Calico, a good-time girl whose desire for expensive gifts results in her boyfriend Dave (Terence Morgan) accumulating unaffordable debts. This fickle femme fatale urges him to rob the office safe even though she's fallen for his brother Johnny (George Baker) by this time, which not only leads to a murder but also to Dave's mental breakdown. Calico, therefore, spins a web of deceit and destruction much like Phyllis in *The Unholy Wife*.

Dors' character in *Passport to Shame* is more sympathetic despite being a bad girl, a glamorous but tough prostitute in a London brothel. Clad in tight, figure-hugging costumes, the star's shapely curves are accentuated here, making her look more than ever like an inflatable sex doll. Despite being a bad girl, Vicki is treated sympathetically and with some respect, the film presenting an unusually frank depiction of prostitution (Bell 2010: 143). Indeed, she becomes a hero when she locks Nick Biaggi (Herbert Lom) in an attic room and sets fire to it in revenge for the disfigurement and suicide of her younger sister. Biaggi subsequently falls to his death from a high window ledge when attempting to escape. Despite this, however, Vicki is not the film's central character, which is Malou (Odile Versois), a young and innocent Parisian waitress who is tricked into coming to London by Aggie (Brenda De Banzie), Biaggi's procuress. Malou soon finds herself trapped in a brothel being groomed as a high-class prostitute or 'special' under Vicki's tutelage, until Johnny (Eddie Constantine) and a mob of taxi-drivers come to her rescue (see Bell 2010: 142–6).

Of these three films, *Passport to Shame* is the one that most fully reveals the contradictions at the heart of Dors' star image. For here she is the very personification of a highly sexualised working girl who is both tough but good-hearted, indomitable but controlled by powerful men, exploited yet independent, purchasable but self-possessed. Nevertheless, *The Long Haul* and *Tread Softly Stranger* gave the actress greater acting opportunities despite being vehicles for male actors in the main role. For instance, although *Tread Softly Stranger* really belongs to George Baker as gambler Johnny Mansell, it contains one of Dors' longest speeches in a dramatic monologue delivered directly to camera. Recalling scenes by Barbara Stanwyck as the peroxide blonde Lily Powers in *Baby Face* (Green 1933) and Joan Blondell as the titular character of *Blondie Johnson* (Enright 1933), who deliver similar confessional speeches to the men they materially and sexually exploit in their bid to escape a life of poverty in Hollywood cinema of the 1930s, this constitutes an established cinematic trope intended to generate empathy for wicked women. In *Tread Softly*, it not only does this but also establishes Calico's backstory; namely the fact that she has made her way out of a slum to gain her position in the world as a good-time girl. While this direct-to-camera confessional monologue begins ironically, it becomes more poignant, allowing Dors to both communicate directly with the audience and elicit a sympathetic hearing at a time when critics and audience were turning against her.

Dors adopts a series of emotions and attitudes during Calico's big speech, from pride to sardonic wit through to pathos and vulnerability. There are several moments here that showcase the actress's versatility; notably when she introduces more irony and humour as Calico recalls the moment she discovered that she was attractive to the opposite sex and that 'legs weren't just to stand on'. Within the bat of an eyelash, she adopts a more soulful attitude to become sincere when talking about how she exploited her talents. After sounding tough and determined, she softens as Calico admits that she never really loved anyone before Johnny. Dors' voice breaks with emotion at this point and her eyelashes flutter before becoming temporarily speechless. Though words visibly form on her lips, no sound emanates, producing an image of self-pity before she pleads with Johnny to believe her, pitifully repeating his name. Segueing from pretense to sincerity, pride to pathos and strength to weakness, Dors revels in the chance to portray such diverse attitudes and emotions while eliciting sympathy for her manipulative yet vulnerable character.

Calico's big speech resembles one in *The Long Haul* when Lynn tells Harry about her sad little life while sitting in a roadside café drinking coffee. Tired of being a Glamour Girl, Lynn seeks sympathy from Harry as the two gaze into each other's eyes across the table, not with desire but understanding, forging a connection. Mature is attentive and largely static as Dors performs the lines that establish the basic details of Lynn's backstory. Throughout this tender scene, the actress avoids making her actions seem calculatedly seductive, establishing her as a very different type of woman to Phyllis Hochen in *The Unholy Wife*. It's true that she places a hand over his at the end of their conversation, when thanking him for being 'sympatico'. However, this isn't the hand of a femme fatale but rather someone who is tentatively reaching out to a man for protection having been brutalised by men in the past. Yet the actress doesn't make this wayward woman seem pathetic either. However desperate she might be to find someone to cling to, she's neither simpering nor childlike.

Dors paints a sensitive and complex portrait of Lynn in *The Long Haul*, depicting her as a woman who, despite being a victim of male abuse, retains sufficient confidence to take the upper hand with a man of Victor Mature's stature. It's Lynn that makes the first move, confiding in Harry, appreciating him without flattering him and initiating sexual congress. Taking her time with every line, while mostly averting her gaze and avoiding any obvious batting of eyelashes, Dors invests her character with goodness and intelligence rather than playing her as weak, silly or manipulative. Like *Tread Softly Stranger*, this film gave the actress more scope to add depth and detail to her characterisation than any movie after 1960. With a few exceptions, she was increasingly required to produce caricatures and stereotypes. Yet even then, Dors rendered the most seemingly artificial role momentarily credible, curious or compelling. This was part of her skill and distinctiveness as a screen performer.

Neither shy nor retiring

As noted in the previous chapter, Diana Dors insisted at the height of her career in 1956 that she only had five years in which to capitalise on her assets before an inevitable decline set in. Dors would have retired as a movie star in 1961 had she stuck to this plan. This was a good plan, one that would have spared her a great deal of humiliation and scorn. It was also one that she could have achieved. By 1961, Dors was married to her second husband, the comedian Dickie Dawson, who became a major TV star in the USA, initially as an actor in the comedy series *Hogan's Heroes* (1965-71) and then as a regular guest on *Rowan & Martin's Laugh-In* (1970-73) and *The New Dick Van Dyke Show* (1973-4), before hosting the popular game show *Family Feud* (1976-85). Together, Dors and Dawson acquired a luxurious house on Angelo Drive in LA's Beverly Hills and had two sons, Mark (1960) and Gary (1962). Everything was in place by 1961 for Diana to retire gracefully from the entertainment business while retaining her celebrity as the wife of a successful TV personality.

Dors had also accomplished most of her professional goals by this time, including the publication of her (largely ghost-written) memoir *Swingin' Dors* (1960) and the production of an album of songs under the same title in 1960. At the end of that year, she appeared briefly in two Hollywood movies, playing a Nazi spy disguised as a sexy military chauffeur in Danny Kaye's comedy *On the Double* (Shevelson 1961) and a jaded chorus girl in David Janssen's gangster film *King of the Roaring '20s* (Newman 1961). Towards the end of 1960, American journalists announced that, 'swinging Dors has rebounded and is back playing not in one, but two top flight movies at once' (Thomas 1960) and that 'Diana's Hollywood career is going full speed' (Finnegan 1960). The truth though was that her tiny roles in *On the Double* and *King of the Roaring '20s* were negligible, while neither film made much of an impression at the box-office.

Shortly after being nominated for three Oscars for *The Trials of Oscar Wilde* (1960), the writer-director Ken Hughes expressed interest in making a movie based on the *Swingin' Dors* memoir to be called 'The Diana Dors Story' (Wise 1998: 267). Had this come off it would have given the thirty-year-old actress the chance to retire gracefully from the cinematic spotlight and spend the rest of her life living in style in Los Angeles, sitting by the pool and driving around her glamorous neighbourhood in her open-topped Cadillac while the nanny took care of her boys and her husband became the family breadwinner. Yet Dors' life took a different turn, one that saw her touring the world with her own stage show in between making television programmes and movies, before leaving her husband and children in California to pursue her acting career on stage and screen in Britain (see Cale 2021: 95–110).

Returning to Britain in 1965, Dors was confronted by an unreceptive press as well as a lack of film work despite the fact that a large injection of American finance had re-stimulated the British film industry. Dors' glamorous persona as an icon of unapologetic conspicuous consumption was now totally out of step with the youth-oriented popular culture of the sixties, which was dominated by street fashion (notably, the mini skirt) that made skinny Jean Shrimpton and waif-life Twiggy the feminine icons of the age. Rita Tushingham was *the* star of British cinema by this time, personifying a new kind of working-class heroine who could take on the world without changing her name and her northern accent (see Williams 2017: 88–110). Meanwhile, Julie Christie was the new blonde on the block, supplanting the 1950s blonde bombshell with a naturalism, low-key sense of style and an underlying sexual confidence that made Dors look like a caricature in a smutty seaside postcard. After hit films like *Billy Liar* (1963) and *Darling* (1965), Christie was offered the female lead opposite Omar Sharif in David Lean's *Doctor Zhivago* (1965), heading a large international cast that included Rod Steiger (see Bell 2016: 26–51).

When David Lean failed to hire her to portray a character in his lavish historical Russian romantic drama, Diana Dors accepted a bit-part in *The Sandwich Man* (1966). Her nameless character in this Michael Bentine comedy was described as 'First Billingsgate Lady'. It consisted of a few lines of dialogue alongside Anna Quayle discussing the relative merits of the TV doctors James Kildare (Richard Chamberlain) and Ben Casey (Vince Edwards), while around them fish are being unceremoniously gutted. Here, Dors' familiar sex symbol image was abandoned for the first time, her trademark blonde hair concealed under a headscarf as part of her dowdy costume. No longer a good-time girl, she was now presented as a drab middle-aged housewife, an early incarnation of the 'battle-axes' she would repeatedly play during the early 1970s. However, Dors' blonde locks reappeared in Richard Johnson's action thriller *Danger Route* (1967), even though it was Carol Linley who was the film's sexiest blonde, especially when appearing naked in a bathtub tantalisingly concealed by soapsuds.

Dors' film career failed to rejuvenate during the late 1960s, although her performance with Hollywood legend Joan Crawford in *Berserk!* (O'Connelly 1967) proved to be a highlight (see Chapter 7). The most bankable female in this movie, however, was neither Crawford nor Dors but Judy Geeson, who had shot to fame as a mini-skirted troublesome teenager in Sidney Poitier's *To Sir, With Love* (Clavell 1967). It was Geeson who subsequently took the leading female role in the action thriller *Hammerhead* (Miller 1968) in which Dors had another minor role. She also had a small part in *Baby Love* (Reid 1969), appearing at the start as a terminally ill middle-aged blonde in the act of committing suicide. The sense that her time as a sex symbol was over was particularly acute here when she reappeared briefly as the dead mother of Linda Hayden's young nymphet in a series of dream sequences and flashbacks without any dialogue, being reduced to a haunting presence, one that refused to go away.

Diana Dors' film career finally appeared to be over when 1969 passed without any film projects for this thirty-eight-year-old actress. In this year, she signed a contract with Yorkshire TV for her own situation comedy. *Queenie's Castle* (1970–72) was written by Keith Waterhouse and ran for three series over the next two years until it was replaced in 1973 by a less successful Dors' vehicle called *All Our Saturdays* (1973) (see Cale 2021: 126–34). *Queenie's Castle* certainly boosted her flagging public profile in Britain but it was her appearance on stage in 1970 with her younger husband Alan Lake that showcased her acting skills. Dors received excellent reviews for her role as a lusty matriarch in Donald Howarth's comedy *Three Months Gone* at the Royal Court Theatre in London, which quickly sold out. After moving to the Duchess Theatre in the West End, this reaffirmed the bankability of her name when playing to capacity crowds (Bret 2010: 209). Yet even this was not enough to gain her anything more substantial than a handful of small movie roles, including Peter Sellers and Goldie Hawn's comedy *There's a Girl in My Soup* (Boulter 1970). After turning forty, however, Dors bucked the trend that rendered mid-life female movie stars redundant. Over the next few years, she played a range of characters in films such as *The Amazing Mr Blunden* (Jeffries 1973) and *Steptoe & Son Ride Again* (Sykes 1973). This included some rather extraordinary housewives, from battle-axe harridans to sex-starved cougars preying on younger males in films such as *The Pied Piper* (Demy 1972), as discussed in Chapter 8.

Although the 1970s were lean years for the British economy, for Dors they provided an abundance of movie roles, her output increasing from three films in 1972 to five films in 1975. This was in spite of a steady drop in cinema attendances and the annual number of British feature films made during these years (Smith 2008: 67). Like many British actors at this time, Dors found gainful employment in horror movies, with small roles in Vincent Price's *Theatre of Blood* (Hickox 1973), Peter Cushing's *Nothing but the Night* (Sasdy 1973) and *From Beyond the Grave* (1974), as well as Jack Palance's *Craze/The Infernal Doll* (Francis 1974) (see Cale 2021: 141–3). However, it was her appearance in a series of soft-core sex films and smutty sex comedies that led to the revival of her stardom in the seventies.

Dors was given top billing in 1972 (for the first time since 1959) by the producer Vernon Becker for her role as the brothel madam and mistress of ceremonies at Maison Margareta in *Swedish Wildcats*. This low-budget soft-core porn film directed by Joe Sarno featured copious amounts of bare flesh, fetish gear, sadomasochism and kitsch cabaret. Her portrayal of Aunt Margareta, who stages live sadomasochistic sex shows for her wealthy clientele at her brothel in Copenhagen, introduced a more explicitly sexualised Dors' persona. Becker also cast her in a smaller role as a brothel madam in *What the Swedish Butler Saw* (Becker 1975), a badly dubbed, X-rated, low-budget sex comedy set in Victorian London. Playing the wheelchair-bound Madam Helen, she instructs the film's virginal protagonist Jack Armstrong (Ole Søltoft) in the art of sex. Later, she persuades him to educate the innocent and puritanical Alice Faversham (Sue Longhurst) by subjecting her to series of sadomasochistic sex acts. As Dors graduated from good-time girl and prostitute to procuress in her two Swedish soft-porn films, she gained more power and authority in roles that exploited her earlier sex symbol status while accommodating her age and experience.

In 1975, Diana Dors' highly sexualised image was exploited in the sex comedies *The Amorous Milkman* (Nesbitt), *Bedtime with Rosie* (Rilla), *Three for All* (Campell) and *Adventures of a Taxi Driver* (Long). This was a peak year in terms of the production and popularity of low-budget comedies with scenarios about people (mostly working-class tradesmen) enjoying constant sexual opportunity in what might otherwise be considered a dull, drab and depressed Britain (Sheridan 2001: 26). Such films were one of the most reliable areas of investment in the British film industry at this time despite making heavy demands upon their audience's stamina – in terms of laughter and libido – with a constant diet of innuendo and soft-core voyeurism. While celebrated in some quarters by cult audiences, seventies British sex comedies have been summarily dismissed by leading film historians as 'ghastly British cinematic abominations' that were not only sexist, homophobic and racist but also 'neither sexy nor comic' (Petley 2001: 210). Nevertheless, many enjoyed longs runs at inner city cinemas across the country and created a new generation of British blonde stars, notably Mary Millington and Sue Longhurst (see Petley 2001 and Hunter 2008).

After receiving second billing for *The Amorous Milkman* in 1975, Dors was given top billing for the female-authored Edwardian sex comedy *Keep It Up Downstairs* (1976). This not only capitalised on the success of *Can You Keep It Up for a Week?* (Atkinson 1974), made by the same company (Pyramid Films, owned by Adair and Kent Walton), but also London Weekend Television's *Upstairs, Downstairs* (1971–5). The latter, a drama series depicting the lives of the aristocratic Bellamy family and their domestic staff, gained a huge national and international following during the early seventies. For *Keep It Up Downstairs*, screenwriter and producer Hazel Adair – who had previously created the BBC TV series *Compact* (1962–5) and the longer running ITV drama serial *Crossroads* (1964–88) – re-imagined life in an English country house to allow masters and servants to live happily together and have sex with each other regularly throughout the day (Sheridan 2001: 160). The protagonists here fornicate with willing partners regardless of class, age, race or gender, demonstrating a nonchalant attitude to the sight of others engaged in the daily round of sexual intercourse and domestic chores. This is a free for all in which everyone is invited to participate, with the exception of Willy Rushton's character Snotty Shuttleworth, a sniveling upstart who has bought up the debts of the impecunious aristocratic Cockshute family.

Keep It Up Downstairs is both a parody of *Upstairs, Downstairs* and a pastiche of the English country house farce in which everyone hides in wardrobes and under beds, steals along corridors late at night and takes their chances with whomever they find on the other side of the bedroom door. As such, it belongs to one of Britain's most popular and perennial theatrical genres, while drawing on bawdier traditions that date back at least as far as the late 1300s, including Geoffrey Chaucer's *The Canterbury Tales* (1387–1400) and Daniel Defoe's *Moll Flanders* (1722). Yet, in other ways, *Keep It Up Downstairs* was steeped in the culture of the mid-1970s despite its 1904 setting, belonging to a free-spirited post-Pill age of unfettered sexuality in which sexual liberation made it harder for young attractive women to fend off male sexual advances. However, rather than explore the film's ideological significance or its reworking of farce conventions for the 1970s, *Keep It Up Downstairs* has been dismissed as 'truly appalling', less apparently for its sexual double standard than for having a 'sub-Carry-On plot' that consists of 'endless innuendoes' (Petley 2001: 213). For Julian Petley, the film's few redeeming features consist of two sex scenes featuring Mary Millington and 'the sheer strangeness of her lesbian threesome in a bathroom' (213).

Hazel Adair's sex comedy is not without merit and Dors supplies one of its funniest moments. This occurs when a young woman starts screaming in the corridor thinking she's seen a ghost and Lord Cockshute (Mark Singleton) interrupts what is presumably his attempt at cunnilingus on Diana Dors' Daisy Dureneck to apologise for hurting her. Dors' Daisy replies impatiently, declaring with a heavy sigh, 'Don't kid yourself, Randy, it's not me who's screaming!' This gave the actress the chance to channel her inner Mae West, which she did again when performing an intimate scene with the actor Simon Brent. When Rogers, the head groom at the Cockshute stables, tells Daisy he doesn't want to forget his place given that she's an honoured guest, Dors sounds more like West than ever when responding with the line, 'If you do, you can always come up to mine!' Playing a former chorus girl named Daisy Daydream who is now the wife of a wealthy American industrialist, Dors shifts continually between a Cockney accent and an American (or trans-Atlantic) one, while remaining at all times sexually desiring and confident in her sexual desirability. As such, she's one of many women in this film (notably Sue Longhurst as Lady Cockshute) who are constantly engaged in trying to satisfy their insatiable sexual desires whilst retaining their dignity and respectability.

Keep It Up Downstairs is a rarity in not only being female authored and produced but also in permitting Dors' character to be sexual without condemning her as a 'tart' (*Tread Softly Stranger*) or a 'slut' (*Berserk!*) or by any other derogatory and misogynistic label. Nor is she punished at the end for being overtly sexual, desiring and promiscuous. In fact, the ending of this film proves to be one of the most satisfactory for any of Dors' film characters. Not only does Daisy remain happily married to her millionaire husband but she also happily marries off her daughter Betsy Ann (Seretta Wilson) to Lord Cockshute's son and sole heir Peregrine (Jack Wild) after he has restored the noble family's flagging fortunes. Moreover, Daisy seduces the butler Percy Hampton (Neil Hallett) in the final scene when he arrives at her bedside with breakfast on a tray. Finding Daisy in Lady Cockshute's bed waiting to be served by him in his inimitable way, Hampton is obliged to perform his duty, which he presumably does as the film's theme song 'Always My Pleasure to Serve, Milady' plays out over the closing credits.

After her starring role and happy ending in *Keep It Up Downstairs*, Dors made just two more films in the 1970s, *Adventures of a Private Eye* (Long 1977) and *Confessions from the David Galaxy Affair* (Roe 1979), dividing her time mostly between television work and publishing autobiographical books (see Cale 2021: 148–50). The latter were cheap paperbacks, full of salacious details and bitchy remarks about co-stars, which exposed many of the more sordid aspects of her life. Priced at 95 pence, these were mostly compilations of anecdotes and opinions using an A to Z format that Dors found easy to write and which sold well with suggestive titles such as *For Adults Only* (1978) and *Behind Closed Dors* (1979), the latter being described on the back cover as a 'racy collection of gossip, hard facts and bawdy reminiscence'.

Despite declaring in the foreword to *For Adults Only* that she had no intention of writing her autobiography until she was eighty in 2011, Dors published her life story under the title *Dors by Diana* in 1981. This £1.60 Futura paperback was presented as the 'first, full story she has ever written of her extraordinary life'. The back cover blurb described 'how, with fame and the luxury of Hollywood stardom, came heartbreak and tragedy – the turbulent marriages, the bitter-sweet love affairs, the broken promises and terrible betrayals', clearly situating Dors' personal history within the realms of popular women's romantic fiction.

Dors' cheap racy books replaced her cheap racy films in the late 1970s, making her the queen of trash by the early eighties. By this time, she had long been associated with what was generally derided as 'low-brow' culture. In the mid-fifties she lacked cultural capital despite her impressive earning power, being considered too starry, too sexy, too driven by material gain and the trappings of success to be taken seriously. Even after proving that she could act in *Yield to the Night*, Dors remained déclassé, more of a sex symbol and Hollywood wannabe than a serious actor (Williams 2017: 65). In the mid-1960s, she was reduced to earning her living performing in working men's clubs, which represented the lowest rung of the entertainment industry after street busking (see Chapter 7). Age and weight-gain further eroded Dors' reputation, while low status genres (namely horror, children's films, sex comedies and soft porn) indicated her lack of cultural capital in the 1970s. Even second wave feminism reduced her to the status of a misogynistic sexual travesty. Within the context of the Women's Liberation Movement, Dors was not just a sex 'object' but also a traitor to her sex.

> Let me state strongly, before we begin, that I am not an advocate of Women's Lib, nor am I the sort of woman who has a deep-rooted fear or dislike of men. On the contrary I adore them, but it is because I have always done so that I feel compelled to write this seemingly 'anti-male' book. (Dors 1981: 7)

While insisting that she was not a feminist, Dors made it perfectly clear on the very first page of her memoir that she believed her life had been lived in 'a man's world' and that, implicitly, many of her failures resulted from having broken patriarchal rules. Meanwhile, her story describes how men controlled her, squandered her earnings, while physically and psychologically abusing her. This was as much a salutary tale as Launder and Gilliat's *Lady Godiva Rides Again* (see Chapter 2), warning of the dangers that lie in store for girls and young women who desire fame and fortune as professional performers and movie stars, especially glamorous girls who hope to trade on their youth and beauty. If these girls had anything to learn from Dors' autobiography, it was to avoid men. Another lesson seemed to be that theatre and television provided greater opportunities for actresses than cinema.

The greatest acting challenge of Dors' later life may well have been her performance on stage as Jocasta in Sophocles' tragedy *Oedipus Tyrannus*, which she gave at the Chichester Festival in 1974 (Bret 2010: 196). Performing opposite the festival's artistic director Keith Michell, she received rave reviews for a part and a play that could hardly have been more different to all the minor roles in horror movies and smutty sex comedies that had become the mainstay of her film career by this time (Cale 2021: 138).

In 1980, Dors performed in four separate TV productions, most notably as the supreme leader of Britain's female militia that subjugates men by forcing them into domestic servitude as floral-frock wearing minions in 'The Worm That Turned' segments of *The Two Ronnies* comedy sketch show. In addition to this, Dors appeared in an adaptation of *Dr. Jekyll and Mr. Hyde* starring David Hemmings, an episode of *Hammer House of Horror* ('Children of the Full Moon' with Christopher Cazenove), as well as the detective drama series *Shoestring* (starring Trevor Eve). Switching between comedy and drama, historical fantasy and contemporary realism, Dors displayed her flexibility and acting range to millions of viewers watching these top-rated TV shows (Cale 2021: 149). The following year, the esteemed theatre director, drama critic and polymath Jonathan Miller cast Dors in a small role as the prostitute Timandra in his television production of William Shakespeare's *Timon of Athens* (1981) starring Jonathan Pryce (150). Three years later, she was cast alongside the much admired and highly acclaimed actress Vanessa Redgrave in Joseph Losey's film version of Nell Dunn's award-winning feminist play *Steaming* (see Chapter 9), which brought her decisively into the feminist fold within months of her death.

From trash to treasure

Diana Dors was more than a distinguished actor when she died in May 1984, having acquired 'national treasure' status (Williams 2017: 78). In part, this stemmed from the fact that all kinds of people liked her, identified with and admired her; including women and men, young and old, gay and straight. This also involved a belated recognition that she was a woman whose intelligence and talent deserved to be taken seriously despite her persistent adoption of an excessively glamorous and overly sexualised femininity. Dors' combination of talent and industriousness, confidence and honesty, versatility and longevity, intelligence and wit, along with her stoicism and strength, made her a rare figure within the history of British entertainment, one whose stature could not be diminished by the paucity of her film roles. The way in which she transcended these to become a major star is impressive. However, this should not obscure the fact Dors left behind some marvelous moments within her motley movie back catalogue, as discussed in the following chapters.

Part two
Acting and performance

Chapter 5

Pseudo-star acting in *Is Your Honeymoon Really Necessary?* (1953)

Is Your Honeymoon Really Necessary? (hereafter, referred to as *Honeymoon*) is a small-scale 80-minute British comedy with all the hallmarks of a B-movie despite its talented Anglo-American cast and distinguished veteran director Maurice Elvey. As explained in Chapter 2, although well on the way to becoming a major movie personality in Britain and the States in 1953, Dors had to wait another two years before she could truly be considered a film star. Consequently, *Honeymoon* wasn't a Dors' star vehicle but rather an ensemble comedy in which the American actor Bonar Colleano received first billing for his role as the main protagonist. Nevertheless, Dors outshone him and everyone else here despite maintaining an understated and naturalistic performance. The twenty-one-year-old actress is spectacular in *Honeymoon*, which is only partly due to her youthful beauty and slender physique. In a leading role, she asserts her star qualities with a supremely self-confident performance. My focus in this chapter is therefore on how Dors performed her role in *Honeymoon* as if she was a major movie star.

The saga of an unnecessarily fraught and farcical honeymoon with two wives

American naval commander Laurie Vining (Bonar Colleano) arrives in England with his new bride Gillian (Diana Decker) only to have his honeymoon gatecrashed by his first wife. The glamorous model Candy Markham (Diana Dors) believes that she's still legally married to Vining on the grounds that his American-obtained divorce is not binding in Britain. Consequently, having moved into the guest room of his hotel suite, she refuses to leave until a once-promised £5,000 settlement is honoured. Vining tries to keep this from his bride, summoning his lawyer Frank Betterton (David Tomlinson) to assist him in getting rid of Candy. It subsequently transpires that the sexually inhibited Frank has always been in love with Candy, who eventually falls for his bumbling boyish charms.

Prior to getting his heart's desire, Frank is repeatedly humiliated. Having been forced to spend a night in a bathtub, for instance, he wakes to find that the taps have been turned on, soaking his borrowed garish pyjamas. Meanwhile, Laurie is exhausted after spending much of the night standing on his head while attempting to avoid his new wife's sexual advances. As Laurie's efforts to resolve his honeymoon crisis become increasingly desperate, he reverts to childish behaviour. This scenario therefore emasculates the two male leads while empowering the two principal females. After seeing through the various deceptions of the men, Candy and Gillian make them suffer for a while as a salutary lesson before finally forgiving them.

Despite the fact that Laurie is a high-ranking officer and Frank is a senior partner in a law firm, both are presented here as boys. Frank's sexual inexperience and insecurity certainly render him infantile. While Laurie is sexually confident and experienced, he behaves throughout in childlike ways. This forces the two Mrs Vinings to assume more adult roles, being patient and understanding but also punishing the boys for their misdemeanors. Candy inflicts Laurie's punishment with good humour and no sense of malice, yet this is no less effective for being delivered in a spirit of fun. Although Candy doesn't gain £5,000 in the end (and is seemingly unconcerned about this), she does have the satisfaction of witnessing Laurie repeatedly squirm. Laurie not only ends up with a headache but also his image as a great womaniser is shattered. After her unconsummated wedding night, Gillian suspects that her husband might be homosexual, suspecting that he deserted her for most of the previous evening to spend time with his wise-cracking gum-chewing and incessantly hungry chauffeur and former wartime batman Hank (Sid James). Consequently, Candy has done more than simply gatecrash her ex-husband's honeymoon, for she has also opened Gillian's eyes to her husband's eccentricity, irresponsibility and immaturity.

If Laurie deserves to suffer for his misdemeanors and broken promises, Frank's punishment seems less justified. Ostensibly, Candy punishes him for his complicity with Laurie. Yet there's also a suspicion that Frank is being punished for his failure to assume the role of sexual partner, husband and provider. Initially depicted as a shy bachelor more preoccupied with his hobby of collecting birdsongs than his profession, Frank might well be judged to have failed to attain adult masculinity. He's certainly emasculated by Candy when she locks him in her room for the night and conceals the key, first down her cleavage and then under her pillow. Trapped, Frank hides in a wardrobe while Candy changes into her nightwear, too embarrassed to see her undress. So one of the less progressive aspects of *Honeymoon* is its suggestion that men like Laurie and Frank need to grow up and assume adult responsibilities, not only as financial providers but also as dominant sexual partners. In the final sequence, therefore, after Candy has accepted his marriage proposal, Frank becomes noticeably more assertive, almost commanding in his new role as a prospective husband.

The more progressive aspects of *Honeymoon* include its depiction of high status males associated with the military and the law as incompetent and childish, as well as the fact that the women they love are much smarter, more sexually confident and always come out on top. It's true that Candy and Gillian display the virtue of patience, which for so long had been upheld as a principal virtue of femininity. It's also true that they are both placed in essentially maternal roles when it comes to dealing with the errant behaviour of Laurie and Frank. While these are traditionally conservative notions of female conduct, Candy and Gillian nevertheless are shown to be the dominant sex in this convoluted scenario. The gender role reversals involved in this may well be amusing and intended to make audiences laugh but they are no less disruptive and radical.

Diana's almost perfect fit

For her role as Candy Markham, Dors was required to do little more than be herself or, more accurately, utilise her developing star persona with her own voice and manner of speaking, her familiar poses, body postures and hairstyle. Although she wasn't a major movie star, Dors performed her role as though she was. Consequently, the performance she produced here could be considered as a type of 'star acting'.

Like most actors working in the commercial film industry, stars usually construct their characters and create their performances by analysing scripts or screenplays, experimenting with different ways of performing their lines, being mostly guided by descriptive passages that indicate how the writer has conceived of the character's appearance and behaviour. Stars may collaborate with an acting coach on big budget films, as well as either a dialogue director or an assistant director, working out performance details in advance of the shoot. On smaller scale productions, however, they may simply devise a performance on their own or with a fellow cast member, further developing this with the director on set. In either case, part of the star's task is to a craft a character for the screen and produce a distinctive set of actions involving physical gestures and vocal inflections that convey both the type of person they are performing (as a recognisable social type) and as a more nuanced and individuated personality.

When playing well-known fictional characters such as Sherlock Holmes, Lady Macbeth, Ebenezer Scrooge and Miss Marple, most stars aim to remain faithful to the author's conception of the character while also making the part their own by introducing some aspect of characterisation and performance that no previous actor has done before. So there is inevitably a balancing act for stars between being true to the author and themselves. Whether the character is well known or not, star actors ordinarily aim to make them credible, so that audiences can believe in them. Through their words and actions, most attempt to convey the intentions of the screenwriter and the director while also expressing what the actor personally believes their character is thinking and feeling at any moment in the film. Yet star actors (as opposed to unknown or little known actors) have their own very distinctive style of performance, sometimes referred to as an 'idiolect'. In most instances, producers pay stars much more than unknown actors because they want them to perform their screen character in their own idiosyncratic way.

In addition to their own unique style of performance, most stars have an 'image' that exists beyond their screen work, including a 'private life' that is written about or exposed in magazines and elsewhere, both exploiting and intensifying public interest in them. Once this image has become desirable to large numbers of people, it becomes a valuable commodity, one that can be bought and sold, as well as lucratively loaned out to film producers. When secured by a producer, a star image can be utilised by a director to create a screen character that is appealing and distinctive. In taking on a particular role in a movie, a star's character not only becomes invested with their own persona but also automatically stands out from all the other characters played by less well-known actors.

By recruiting Diana Dors to play Candy Markham in *Honeymoon* in 1953, David Dent intended this character to stand out from the rest of the cast. When directing Dors in this role, Maurice Elvey could rely on the fact that whatever she did before his camera or said into his microphone would make a strong impact upon an audience. Dent and Elvey would also have expected Dors to imbue her screen character with elements of her own star image, one that was gaining increasing favour with audiences in Britain and the USA in 1953. When performing Candy Markham, Dors was able to draw on her own personal experiences as a photographic model. The filmmakers, meanwhile, could exploit her stylish peroxide blonde hairstyle and her reputation for being sexually assertive, smart, sassy, quick-witted and confident, as well as her association with glamorous clothes. Consequently, various components of the Dors' star image make Candy credible as a glamorous, clever, attractive, seductive and successful young woman. To achieve this, the actress didn't need to change the way she ordinarily spoke, moved or posed. Instead, Diana Dors fitted the role of Candy Markham almost perfectly, her image being well suited to both Candy's social type as a glamour model and her personality. Yet, in other ways, this screen character departs from Dors' image, mostly notably in terms of her attitudes to money and men.

Diana's oft-reported desire for money is implicated as Candy's motivation for disrupting her first husband's second honeymoon. However, it later becomes clear that Candy's actions are motivated by a desire to punish Laurie for his broken promises rather than financial gain. A character closer to Dors' reputation at this time would be one driven by a desire for large amounts of money and would have been frustrated by not gaining this at the end. Similarly, while Diana was known to have a strong attraction to bad boys (including thugs and criminals), Candy ultimately falls for the boyish and innocent charms of Frank, who (as played by David Tomlinson) is not Dors' type of man at all. Yet it's precisely in such departures from the established public image of Diana Dors that Candy Markham resides as a character in her own right. The gap between actor and character – however large or small – provides pleasure for an audience. So while audiences can enjoy the spectacle of Dors behaving *as Dors* on screen, they can derive just as much pleasure from seeing her assume a different identity as someone who is distinct from any other character she had played up until this time or from her established public persona.

The simultaneous existence of a strong resemblance between actress and character with a discernable gap between the two is critical here and, for Paul McDonald, is a fundamental feature of 'star acting'; 'It is this tension between story and show, or between the representation of character and the presentation of the star, that forms the basic contradiction of film star acting', he writes (2012: 170). In his essay 'Story and Show', McDonald investigates how well-known actors create distinctive characters on screen that audiences can believe in by being 'spectacular', on the one hand, and both subsuming and utilising (or showing) aspects of their own personality, on the other (2012: 170–71). What is particularly pertinent to understanding Dors' performance in *Honeymoon* is the idea that an actor typically draws directly on two things when bringing a character to life on screen: (1) their knowledge of the world (and how different kinds of people usually behave), and (2) their own thoughts, feelings, gestures, behaviours and personality. In the process of doing the latter, an actor both subsumes and utilises (or shows) aspects of his or her own personality. Another way to describe this process is that actors can either go 'into character' as a form of disguise or put themselves (their personality) into their character as a form of (self) revelation.

Barry King has provided another way of conceptualising this with his terms 'impersonation' and 'personification'. In his essay 'Articulating Stardom,' he used the word 'impersonation' to describe the effect of a well-known actor's disappearance when playing a part, while employing 'personification' to denote the opposite, when a star retains his or her own established image while performing a character (King 1991: 168). King's distinction has proven useful for distinguishing between theatre and film performance, character acting and star acting, as well as enabling film scholars to differentiate between performances in which an actor goes 'into character' or remains recognisably themselves on screen at all times. 'What King's opposition boils down to', writes Paul McDonald, 'is the contrast between two performance principles: impersonation is based on difference and discontinuity, whereas personification rests on continuities and sameness' (2012: 172). While King recognises the value of personification in cinema, McDonald goes further by regarding it as a prerequisite for stardom. 'By foregrounding actor over the character, it is easy to see how personification can be judged to be a basic requirement of star acting' even if it leads to many stars being criticised for just being themselves in one role after another (McDonald 2012: 172). Despite such negative criticism, the rewards of personification include higher salaries as producers are prepared to pay more for actors that can bring their unique image and acting style to a role (173).

Yet, for Paul McDonald, star acting is never just a matter of personification given that 'the star is always required to perform the specific demands of the story' (173). Consequently, he conceives of impersonation and personification 'as poles on a continuum across which any film performance may be positioned' rather than as 'absolutely opposed principles' (173). This is an important distinction. I would certainly argue that Diana Dors created screen performances that simultaneously exploited her recognisable persona with something essentially unique to the specific part she's playing in a particular film. So, although she may appear to be behaving on screen in ways that audiences had grown accustomed to seeing as idiosyncratic – featuring her own hair and makeup, clothes, voice, accent, phraseology, movements, gestures, poses, postures, expressions and looks – the actress would always conceal some aspects of herself and go into character to some extent whenever she played a part. If, as McDonald suggests, film acting typically operates across a spectrum – with personification at one end and impersonation at the other (and with star acting mostly existing on the personification side) – then Dors' performance can be considered to be star acting in *Honeymoon* even if she wasn't the film's main star or widely considered to be a major star at the time.

Not a character actor

Unlike stars, character actors are commonly associated with exaggeration, particularly over-playing in short scenes to gain maximum attention. As Ernest Mathijs has observed in his essay 'From Being to Acting,' character actors specialise in a small repertoire of roles, their expertise saving writers and directors a lot of time and effort (2012: 143). By playing more or less the same type in one role after another (for instance, policemen, teachers, doctors, maids, butlers, thugs, etc.), these actors require relatively little direction, being recognised as experts in playing their particular type. Despite their expertise, however, character actors rarely get the star treatment in terms of screen time, close-ups, the best lighting or the much coveted position at the centre of the screen, which is ordinarily reserved for the star and can therefore be thought of as the 'star slot'. Mathijs argues that many character actors compensate for this with a high degree of overplaying in order to be noticed, employing what he calls 'vivid expressiveness' (143).

Sarah Thomas, in her essay '"Marginal moments of spectacle": Character Actors, Cult Stardom and Hollywood Cinema', notes that because character actors' appearances in films are restricted in terms of space and time, 'their acting reflects this limited spacetime in its broadly excessive style', one that renders them highly visible and entertaining to some audiences (2013: 43). Indeed, many prove adept at stealing scenes from the stars they are employed to support. Common 'scene stealing' antics include the ostentatious use of props, a particular set of mannerisms, a style that is more formalistic than naturalistic, swift shifts in emotional register and a distinctive voice that maintains the presence of the supporting actor even when the star's image dominates the screen (Thomas 2013: 44–9).

When making brief appearances in films such as *The Shop at Sly Corner* (1946) and *Oliver Twist* (1948), Diana Dors may have needed to use the techniques associated with character acting. Yet she mostly avoided overplaying and more formalistic devices, using muted naturalistic performances instead, as explained in Chapters 1 and 2. More often than not, she relied on her distinctive voice and an increasingly spectacular image to ensure that she gained attention with brief moments in films like *It's Not Cricket* (1949) and *The Great Game* (1952). This may have been because she considered herself to be a star even when playing small supporting roles, although it's more likely that this was because she believed that she would become a star if she acted like one at all times.

Dors didn't need to overact to be noticed when performing a leading role in *Honeymoon* as this gave her a considerable amount of screen time and a preponderance of medium-close and close shots. What's noticeable here is that she uses a far less demonstrative style of acting than her co-stars. Despite playing the main protagonist, Bonar Colleano performs with exaggerated posturing and vividly expressive facial gestures, bordering on dumbshow in places, including pointing and mimicking. At times he becomes so emphatic that his performance borders on caricature. Meanwhile, Dors makes Candy seem calm and in control throughout this fraught scenario by remaining resolutely subdued, especially when Colleano's character becomes confused, excited and overtaken by panic. Whatever the situation, Dors consistently underplays with a series of small telling looks, expressions, gestures, poses and intonations that seem more incidental than extended, leaving the film's leading man to express himself much more vividly with broader, cruder and more ostentatious actions that turn him into a character actor.

After Laurie Vining has tried unsuccessfully to manhandle Candy physically out of his hotel suite, Dors rapidly regains her composure and refuses to leave without £5,000 in cash, which she demands with a calm voice and an outstretched hand. When an astonished Vining declares that he doesn't have such large sums of money lying around, Dors places her hands on her hips (as can be seen in Figure 5.1). This conveys Candy's resolve and her refusal to budge. At the same time, it enhances the star's spectacular qualities, emphasising her shapely physique – notably her slim waist and ample bosom. Even though Colleano occupies the star slot here at the centre of the frame, it's Dors who attracts the gaze of her two male co-stars and the audience. She's certainly the most spectacular figure on screen when adopting this pose, which had become one of her trademarks by 1953. While enhancing her spectacular qualities, this same pose expressed Candy's determination to stand her ground with little exertion on Dors' part.

Figure 5.1 Diana Dors as Candy Markham in a screen shot from *Is Your Honeymoon Really Necessary?* (Elvey 1953) teaching her former husband Laurie Vining (Bonar Colleano) a lesson, while his former batman Hank (Sid James) helplessly looks on. (Junofilms.com, last accessed 04/02/21.)

Such instances create a palpable sense of Dors drifting through *Honeymoon* without having to do much more than be herself. This could be read as the actress not really trying. Yet this conclusion would ignore the fact that she was playing the part with a subtlety and naturalism characteristic of most major Hollywood movie stars. Rather than execute elaborate physical movements, even when her co-stars adopt a hyper mode of exaggerated performance, Dors typically does something smaller, like raise an eyebrow. Confident in the knowledge that she can command the attention of the camera, she tones everything down, achieving maximum impact with minimal effort.

Diana Dors remains both poised and provocative throughout *Honeymoon*. By imbuing her gestures and looks with dignity, assurance and intelligence, she establishes her character's status as a woman with brains as well as beauty, while simultaneously insisting on her own status as a star actor. Even if the film has all the hallmarks of a second rate low-budget British programme-filler, Dors' pseudo-star performance contends that she deserves better than this. Consequently, in the process of bringing Candy Markham to life, Diana Dors shines brightly as someone whose value and skills far exceed the material she's working with at this stage of her career, not only asserting her competency as a performer of screen comedy but also proclaiming her potential to become a major Hollywood star, if given half a chance.

Chapter 6

A marriage of method and style in *The Unholy Wife* (1957)

The Unholy Wife features Diana Dors in one of her most unsympathetic roles as Phyllis Hochen, an unfaithful wife with no qualms about her husband being executed for a murder she's committed, as well as a neglectful mother who resents her only child from the moment he's born. Once life with the man she's married for security has become tedious, Phyllis plots to kill her husband Paul. Having mistakenly shot his best friend, she frames Paul for this, securing a conviction that sentences him to death. As a bad wife, negligent mother and an all-round wicked woman, Phyllis Hochen is presented in this Technicolor film noir as nothing less than a monstrous incarnation of evil. The task of embodying such a character was no mean feat given that the actress needed to foreground her wickedness without turning her into a grotesque caricature since she needed to elicit sympathy when Phyllis finds redemption in religion at the very end of the film. As discussed in this chapter, this was made more challenging for a British actress working with numerous American Method actors that not only used a range of techniques such as improvisation and 'affective memory' but also deemed the work of their colleagues from across the Atlantic to be old-fashioned, superficial and unemotional.

Diana Dors' performance in her American crime melodrama displays as much composure and control as in her British farce *Is Your Honeymoon Really Necessary?* (Elvey 1953) despite her character being very different and highly unsympathetic. Consolidating her signature style or idiolect, she redeployed her trademark postures when playing an archetypal femme fatale in *The Unholy Wife* (Farrow 1957), while also adapting her acting style to the techniques of the Method actors performing with her.

Analysis of several scenes of this critically underrated movie reveals just how versatile the British star was when working in Hollywood in 1956.

Method and style

John Farrow's casting of Diana Dors and Rod Steiger in the roles of Phyllis and Paul Hochen enabled the producer-director to capitalise on the vogue for both blonde bombshells and male Method actors. While the two stars had received praise for the realism and psychological complexity of their screen performances – Steiger for *On the Waterfront* (Kazan 1954) and Dors for *Yield to the Night* (Lee Thompson 1956) – they were very different kinds of actor. Farrow could exploit this difference to suggest that the marriage depicted in *The Unholy Wife* was one made in hell rather than heaven.

From the moment they appear on screen together, it's clear that Mr and Mrs Hochen are incompatible. Having entered the shot just as Steiger has squeezed a grape and cast it aside, Dors gives him a handkerchief and then strikes a classic Dorsian pose with her hand on her hip. To emphasise her character's frustration, she ripples her fingers just below the belt at her waist while twizzling a stick in her right hand (as seen in Figure 6.1).

Figure 6.1 A screen shot of Diana twizzling her stick alongside a grape-eating Rod Steiger in *The Unholy Wife* (Farrow 1957). (YouTube, last accessed 09/02/2021.)

Although this is a long piece of straw, her handling of it makes it look like a cane. Whatever Phyllis is feeling here, the actress remains calm and composed. Meanwhile, her co-star is all noise and motion, constantly walking and talking, while popping one grape after another into his mouth. This makes it hard to hear what he's saying, especially as he speaks quickly in a high-pitched voice with very little projection. The fact that he states that his neighbour Gino Verdugo is his friend three times in quick succession suggests that he's improvising his dialogue rather than sticking to the script.

Steiger repeatedly looks down at his legs after spitting grape pips out of his mouth, checking that he hasn't messed up his chinos. He does this without hesitating, as though it's a reflex, which makes his behaviour here look natural. Indeed, none of his actions seem to be consciously orchestrated for the camera, everything appearing to have occurred spontaneously as the scene was being shot. In contrast, Dors not only seems much more purposeful in her movements and poses but also regularly steps out of character to assert her own star identity with her familiar postures and looks. These include her hand on hip pose, sulky and sultry pout, as well as her arms folded across her chest posture with her fingers positioned vertically pointing upwards. These are the actress's default methods for conveying such things as impatience, irritation, frustration, resistance and determination.

Many star actors use a recognisable and idiosyncratic set of bodily gestures or idiolect to impart more of themselves into a role and make it their own (see Drake 2004: 74). Dors certainly does this throughout *The Unholy Wife*, which helps to humanise her character. By incorporating aspects of her own distinctive screen persona, the star offsets some of the more monstrous aspects of Phyllis Hochen that derive from her being an archetypal *femme fatale*. When making this film in 1956, Dors was well placed to transform a man-made female character designed to illicit indignation and contempt into an icon of feminine strength and stoicism. Despite her crimes and failings as a wife and mother, Dors makes Phyllis stand proud, whether she has her hands placed firmly on her hips or her arms folded across her chest. In such poses, she seems undaunted by her fate, ready to confront whatever comes next.

Yet Dors wasn't the only actor in *The Unholy Wife* with an idiosyncratic set of mannerisms given that, as Steve Vineberg writes, 'Rod Steiger has the most instantly recognizable style of any of the Actors Studio performers' (1991: 237). His voice alone was immediately recognisable, with its 'honey-coated' tones, 'weirdly energized whine' and staccato rhythm (237). Vineberg even notes that a 'melodramatic tremolo' at the end of a line is a major Steiger trademark, one that the actor typically builds up 'to a blasting crescendo' (237). Meanwhile, his physical bulk produced a very distinctive acting style when he used his 'big, sagging frame and his mouth muscles' to underscore the sadness, impatience and annoyance of his characters. As Steiger often used his weight and bulk to convey a fierce excitement, even frenzy, Vineberg describes him as 'superanimated' (237). Interestingly, one of the consequences of Steiger's overly animated performance style is the sense of him visibly acting, overdoing things, overplaying with gestures, movements and expressions that are larger than life, histrionic and excessive. Indeed, Vineberg calls him 'an incorrigible ham, a terrifically gifted one, with a penchant for indulging his own delight in Method trickery' (237). If this is an apt description, then it suggests that Steiger's hammy qualities may well have undermined the naturalism created by his use of improvisation and reflexive reactions.

Rod Steiger's staccato, light and tremulous voice in *The Unholy Wife* can be perceived as part of the idiolect that he brought to many of his film roles rather than something created uniquely for the role of Paul Hochen. These are effective here, however, precisely because his familiar speech patterns contrast so strikingly with Dors' clear, smooth, deep and steady voice to highlight the couple's unsuitability. At the same time, Steiger's highly animated actions make Dors seem all the more poised. Yet beneath her composed demeanour, the actress was thrown into a state of high excitement when working with her American co-star, as she recalls in her memoir *Dors by Diana*:

> To find myself interested in the art of acting again, to watch his brilliance as we worked together, inspired new and greater artistic heights within me. I had to draw on everything I could to compete against his talent. (1981: 161)

Dors' quick wit no doubt enabled her to compete with Steiger and react immediately to his improvisations, although it must have been disconcerting each time he departed from the screenplay. Whenever he produced a bit of business with a prop on the spur of the moment or performed an action that hadn't been rehearsed or blocked out in advance of the recording, Dors needed to be highly alert and ready to react. As her main co-star, Steiger presented her with a host of challenges, yet so did Tom Tryon in the major supporting role of San Sanders when using methods derived from Sanford Meisner at the Neighbourhood Playhouse in New York. Even Marie Windsor, who played the small supporting role of the prostitute Gwen, utilised techniques taught to her by the Russian expat acting teacher Maria Ouspenskaya, which she herself had inherited from her mentor Konstantin Stanislavsky at the Moscow Art Theatre. Yet what made *The Unholy Wife* so challenging for Dors was that all these proponents of the Method had been taught to scorn the working methods of British actors.

The disparagement of what was called an 'English School of Acting' by America's leading Method instructors has been well documented. For instance, Foster Hirsch describes Lee Strasberg's condemnation of this as 'not humanity or reality' while recording Stella Adler's remark about English actors not bothering with emotion (1984: 219). Virginia Wright Wexman, meanwhile, has argued that a 'British school of performance' was characterised by Method proponents as an external technique (which emphasised appearance through makeup and costume) combined with verbal dexterity (2004: 128).

The idea that English actors like Dors had been trained to speak their lines nicely without emotion is patently ridiculous, as is the very idea of a coherent English or British school of acting. Most actors in Britain during the early to mid 20th century acquired a mixed bag of performance techniques through an informal education as they progressed from school plays to amateur dramatics, repertory theatre to pantomime, variety shows to radio plays, live television to cinema. Performing in modern comedies and classical drama, serious drama and farce in large theatres in London's West End and small provincial ones, British actors encountered all kinds of influences, including French, German, Italian, Greek, Russian *and* American. If anything characterised British acting, it was heterogeneity, which enabled actors in Britain to perform all types of drama in all kinds of places.

Most actors trained in America also acquired a mixed bag of skills and techniques throughout the first half of the 20th century, drawing on a diverse heritage that incorporated many different forms of performance, including Yiddish theatre (Baron 2016: 66). Many leading acting teachers in the USA originated in Europe and brought their own nation's traditions with them, adapting these to the new environments, industries and audiences that they encountered in the States. Acting schools in America incorporated teachers, theories and practices from all over the world, including Britain, as Cynthia Baron has explained (2016: 94–7).

Method acting, on the other hand, was drawn specifically from Russia and the Soviet Union, notably the theories, teachings and experiments of Konstantin Stanislavsky, who brought a group of talented actors from the Moscow Art Theatre to the USA in 1923. This included Richard Boleslavsky and Maria Ouspenskaya, who remained thereafter to set up the Laboratory Theatre – later known as The American Laboratory Theatre – in New York (Baron, 2016: 97–105). Among their students were Stella Adler and Lee Strasberg, who formed Group Theatre along with Harold Clurman and Cheryl Crawford in 1931, creating an ensemble theatre company that used Stanislavsky's system in an adapted form (Baron 2016: 118–31). Over time their approach to acting became known as the 'Method' and was intended to be authentically American despite its Russian roots (Baron 2016: 71–3). It's ironic that the polarisation of something called 'Classical British' and 'American Method' acting has led to the former being marked out as formal and the latter as informal, given that Method acting involves a much more formalised set of practices and theories.

Criticised for being 'poised, formal and overly articulate', British and British-derived acting techniques were condemned by Strasberg, Adler and others, who insisted that Method acting was not only authentically American but also more physical, spontaneous, intense and emotional (Baron 2016: 72). For many advocates of the Method, actions should always speak louder than words, despite all the shouting by male characters that came to epitomise the style. While beauty was abhorrent (especially the beauty of fine language eloquently delivered), ugliness was equated with realism (Hirsch, 1984: 220). As Foster Hirsch observes in *A Method to their Madness*, British acting was set up as an anathema for the Method proponents, particularly at the Actors Studio in New York (1984: 220).

In his capacity as the Director of the Actors Studio from 1949, Strasberg made a deep impression upon successive generations of American actors working in theatre, television and film, including Marilyn Monroe, James Dean, Eva Marie Saint and Rod Steiger. Many of the techniques associated with the Method had been adopted in Hollywood by 1956, especially after Elia Kazan's *On the Waterfront* (1954) won no less than eight Oscars in 1955, including Best Actor in a Leading Role (Marlon Brando), Best Actress (Eva Marie Saint) and Best Director (Kazan). For this celebrated movie, Kazan made a point of hiring Actors Studio-trained performers in order to showcase Method acting techniques such as 'affective memory', which involves the actors substituting their own feelings for those of the characters they are playing in order to portray powerful emotional states (Wright Wexman 2004: 131).

In a very short time, Method actors became major Hollywood stars, including Rod Steiger, who gained international stardom following his Oscar-nominated supporting role in *On the Waterfront*. His success owed much to his association with Strasberg and Kazan, who had not only helped him acquire his acting technique but also influenced his attitudes towards acting and actors in general. There's every chance that Strasberg, Kazan and Steiger would have dismissed Diana Dors as a typical 'Classical British' actor, condemning her for speaking too eloquently, appearing too manicured and holding herself with too much poise. Yet, rather than embody some specific kind of Classical British acting technique, Dors' style was essentially hybrid and heavily influenced by Hollywood. As discussed in the following section, for *The Unholy Wife* she even incorporated some Method devices alongside more formalistic features to render her performance both emotionally charged and stylish.

In tune with Tryon

While Dors' actions are noticeably composed and contained in her scenes with Rod Steiger, her performances with Tom Tryon as Phyllis' lover San Sanders are more animated and intense. Although this is a passionate relationship, Dors retains a sense of control here to indicate her character's manipulative nature. The confident, self-possessed and gently teasing qualities of her speech, for instance, evoke a woman in command of her emotions even when they run high. When Dors takes Tryon's head in her hands to pull him into a kiss (with an accompanying saxophone playing a slow sultry refrain suggestively on the soundtrack), there's little doubt that Phyllis is in charge.

It's clear from the moment that San first appears skulking in the shadows of the dark hallway of the Hochen house that Phyllis finds him irresistible and can't keep her hands off him. Here, Dors runs her fingers across Tryon's shoulders like she's playing a piano. Her right hand lingers on his shoulder, massaging it gently and assessing his strength, while she gazes admiringly at him, seemingly enjoying the feel and sight of his muscles. Her bejewelled fingers are spread open and well lit, standing out against the blackness of her co-star's clothing. As can be seen in Figure 6.2, Dors' hand resembles a large spider crawling over the man's body. Unable to resist, he kisses her passionately after

Figure 6.2 A screen shot of Dors with her spidery fingers crawling over Tom Tryon in *The Unholy Wife* (Farrow 1957). (YouTube, accessed 09/02/2021.)

mumbling something indistinct, working his head into hers, casting a shadow across her face as he succumbs to her lips and mouth.

While Tryon's kiss pushes Dors' head back, her hand climbs up and rests on his shoulder. She's now enfolding him into her body, drawing him in. Any resistance on his part is given up in this moment of oneness. Their faces and bodies burrow into each other as well as into the dark shadows enfolding them. As they twist and turn, Dors' golden hair comes back into the light just before the couple momentarily disentangle themselves. Tryon instantly buries his face in her neck, audibly kissing her skin, from her collarbone up to the area behind her earlobe.

Consumed by darkness, the only distinguishable feature is Dors' right hand and wrist as it slides across the back of Tryon's neck. He whispers indistinctly upon a heavy sigh and then asks if they can get out of the house. After discussing the possibility of murder so that they can be together, Phyllis escorts San to the door. On the threshold, she produces a series of heavy sighs before running her hand over Tryon's back, once more applying the spiderwoman's caress. When she arranges to see him again, San plays hard to get despite being plainly in the palm of her hand. After his departure, Dors closes the door and turns around very slowly to face the camera, raising her hand up to her neck, indicating that she's literally up to her neck in this. A brief look of anxiety dissolves back into sexual longing as her hand caresses the lower part of her neck, resting momentarily on her collarbone, presumably recalling Tryon's kisses upon that same spot. Finally, she adopts a more determined look, her eyes glaring as a plan forms in her mind, just before switching off the lamps in the hallway.

Whereas Dors' first scene with Rod Steiger in the Californian sunshine was all about contrast and incompatibility, this scene with Tom Tryon in the shadows establishes the connection between Phyllis and her lover. A rootless man, San Sanders is an independent wanderer like herself. Physically strong and attractive, he uses his sex appeal to get what he wants. Being a performer in a touring rodeo, San is the very opposite of Paul – nomadic rather than rooted but also lithe, toned, dark, young, handsome and deep voiced. He's the kind of man that Phyllis desires and admires. Yet, while fascinated by Phyllis, San clearly doesn't want to be possessed by anyone. More of a wild colt than a workhorse, he isn't going to let anyone tie him down. This is the essential conflict between the lovers. Otherwise, as their body language suggests in the scene described above, they are not only one – in tune with each other – but also entangled.

The relationship between Phyllis and San is beautifully and powerfully conveyed with an exciting eroticism in their first scene that draws the audience into this fraught but highly charged association. This man and this woman may not trust each other, yet they simply can't leave one another alone. To achieve the effect of a strong and compulsive relationship, each actor needed to perform intimately with the other's body, while reacting to one another's looks, sounds and actions without hesitation.

Tryon was used to performing in tune with his co-actors at the Neighborhood Playhouse in New York City since, as David Krasner writes, Sanford Meisner's teaching there was designed to encourage 'ensemble interplay, or communion' by focusing on 'subtextual dialogue' (2000: 145). This involved putting actors into 'a spontaneous exchange in a jazz-like atmosphere of action and reaction' while encouraging them to treat the audience as a 'scene-partner' (146). This explanation perfectly describes the interplay of Dors and Tryon in their first scene together where the significance lies more in their body language than their verbal dialogue. Without Tryon's training at the Neighborhood

Playhouse, Dors seems to have understood and responded effectively to her co-star's working methods, matching them without any kind of reservation, hesitancy or uncertainty. While working intimately together, the two actors draw the audience into their personal performance space to create this sensual scene of suspicion and yearning, control and abandonment, detachment and surrender.

Yet those spidery hands of Dors suggest something more premediated at work here too, especially when using Tryon's shoulders as a piano keyboard. This has all the hallmarks of a thought-out 'bit of business' designed to convey to the audience how manipulative Phyllis is being. It depicts San as putty in Phyllis's hands while indicating that she's constantly coaxing and teasing rather than sincere. Using these spider-like hands, Dors also renders her character an evil woman as well as a sexual and seductive one. As an archetypal spiderwoman, Phyllis flatters, tempts and seduces but also controls, bending the deep-voiced strongman to her will.

Combining a Meisner-like Method technique of ensemble acting with a more stylised set of hand gestures – which could well have been drawn from German Expressionist cinema as much as American film noir – Dors' performance is not only impressive but also composite. The power and artistry of this scene reside equally in Dors' ability to adjust to and match Tryon's Method performance and augment it with something more stylish and formalistic. In so doing, she exemplifies the hybrid nature of British film acting in the mid 20th century, one that enabled actors to be flexible and versatile when developing performances and characterisations for the screen, even when working in new and foreign contexts alongside colleagues trained in more specific and formalised systems.

To ascribe Dors' performance in *The Unholy Wife* to some typically British school or style and write it off as being poised, verbose and unemotional would ignore her capacity to react spontaneously and intuitively to her co-actor during her intimate scenes with Tom Tryon. Although Dors was far from being a Method actor, she was certainly capable of incorporating some techniques commonly associated with Method acting, as she appears to have done in her RKO crime melodrama. In so doing, the British star demonstrated her versatility as an actor even if very few critics were prepared to acknowledge this when the film was eventually released in 1957.

Chapter 7

Exploiting her nascent has-been status in *Berserk!* (1967)

Diana Dors joined the ranks of the 'has-beens' in the 1960s, notably when cast in a supporting role in Joan Crawford's British thriller *Berserk!* (O'Connelly 1967). Working with one of Hollywood's great comeback queens, she discovered how post-peak stardom imposed a challenging set of demands upon actresses but also gave them some unique opportunities within the margins of mainstream cinema. American producer Herman Cohen and British producer-turned-director Jim O'Connelly allowed Dors to retain her sex symbol image in *Berserk!*. Yet there's more than a hint of mockery about the way she's presented here as a rumour-mongering magician's assistant who refuses to shut her big mouth even at the bitter end.

Dors was at the lowest point of her career when she made this film in 1966. Just ten years after the peak of her stardom and a year after leaving Los Angeles to take her chances as an ageing sex symbol in Britain, the thirty-five-year-old was reduced to singing, joking and telling stories against herself in working men's clubs in some of the roughest parts of England. Here, she was confronted by 'audiences of men heckling me over pints of beer', as she later recalled in *Dors by Diana* (1981: 248). She also described in her autobiography how financial necessity had forced her to prostitute her talent by 'peddling a screen name that had once been big; enduring shouts of "Get 'em off" or "Show us your tits"' (249). Once envied by women and adored by men around the world, Dors was now little more than a target for misogynistic verbal abuse, for which she was mostly paid cash-in-hand.

Dors risked further humiliation when signing on to do Cohen's *Berserk!* even though the producer had a good track record of creating lucrative movies on a shoestring, including *I Was a Teenage Werewolf* (Fowler Jr 1957) and *A Study in Terror* (Hill 1965). The fact that Cohen had hired some talented actors to support Joan Crawford and secured a distribution deal with Columbia Pictures suggested that this exploitation thriller might become a hit and, as such, help Dors regain her footing in the film industry. Sadly, although the film's publicity claimed that *Berserk!* would challenge an audience's ability to withstand a series of horrifying events, it was neither truly terrifying nor terrifically trashy, making it a fairly disappointing experience for most devotees of cult cinema.

For star scholars, however, *Berserk!* is an illuminating film, notably for the way it treats its fading stars Joan Crawford and Diana Dors differently. Given that it was made when both women were widely considered to be 'over the hill', the filmmakers could easily have subjected them to constant ridicule. Indeed, any self-respecting exploitation filmmaker would have forced them to deliver an extreme performance of self-delusion, fear, shock, confusion and anguish. Convention, after all, dictates that fading stars should be goaded into presenting nerve-shattering portraits of their former selves under duress to create distorted and diminished versions of themselves, enabling both jeering and disgusted audiences to mock, scorn and pity them. While its title suggests otherwise, *Berserk!* refrains from the excesses and cruelties of most low-budget horror movies.

Herman Cohen's post-peak Crawford vehicle reveals less about the exploitation of defunct stars and more about the attempt to re-ignite interest in them. Yet these two aspects of exploitation cinema are not mutually exclusive and, as I hope to demonstrate in this chapter, the conflicting ambitions of dignifying and demeaning a faded star operate here. The curious mixture of admiration and contempt that Crawford and Dors inspire in *Berserk!* makes for an unsettling and ambiguous cinematic experience even if ultimately it fails to truly shock or horrify. Analysis of several of Dors' key scenes illustrates the kinds of performance decisions actresses face when working in exploitation thrillers as a 'has-been'.

The expendability of experienced entertainers

Berserk! gave Diana Dors her biggest film role in the 1960s, for which she received third billing after Joan Crawford and the American television actor Ty Hardin. It also gave her the chance to perform with one of Hollywood's most glamorous and resilient drama queens four years after her comeback movie *What Ever Happened to Baby Jane?* (Aldrich 1962). By 1966, however, Crawford had become mired in low-budget shockers that were undermining her credibility as an actress. In *Berserk!* she took on the role of Monica Rivers, the owner of a traveling circus whose performers are being murdered. Following the gruesome death of a tightrope walker during the film's sensational pre-title sequence, Monica becomes a prime suspect, especially when the killings prove good for business by increasing audiences and box-office takings.

Another major suspect is Frank Hawkins (Hardin), who Monica hires as the victim's replacement. After becoming romantically involved with his boss, Frank persuades her to give him a share of the business, much to the dismay of Monica's daughter Angela (Judy Geeson), who appears halfway through the film having been expelled from a private boarding school. Angela subsequently becomes a knife-thrower's assistant shortly before being revealed as a homicidal maniac with abandonment issues, one who stabs Frank in the back during his act. Having made a hysterical confession, Angela runs out into a nocturnal thunder storm, trips over a cable and is electrocuted, forcing Joan Crawford to grieve over her lifeless body for the full duration of the credit sequence as the rain lashes down – presumably, a reminder that it never rains but it pours.

The fact that Angela was away at boarding school when the first two murders are committed only makes an already unlikely scenario even more improbable. Yet this adds to the overall fun of a movie in which Joan Crawford plays a circus owner in a succession of glamorous costumes, including high-heeled shoes that would make walking on grass a constant challenge. The interior of her beautifully appointed caravan, designer jewellery and elaborate hairdo are all part of the star's glamorous identity rather than Monica's itinerant lifestyle. Crawford's portrayal makes little concession to realism and she plays her character as a high-powered businesswoman struggling to manage a disgruntled company of performers that are being lead towards insurrection by the magician Lazlo (Philip Madoc) and his assistant/wife Matilda (Diana Dors).

Matilda is the main thorn in Monica's side, especially when spreading malicious rumours about her. The tension between these two strong women is evident from the start and foregrounded when Crawford's Monica calls Dors' Matilda a 'slut' and a 'miserable ingrate'. From this moment on the battle lines between the two are drawn, promising much more drama to come, possibly even a catfight. Yet, Monica is not prepared to physically fight Matilda. Instead, she shows her strength and authority with a firm voice and a steely glare, Crawford presenting Monica as a woman of steel – determined, independent and unbeatable. She's also a survivor, being the only one of the main characters to be still standing as the credits roll, since those played by Michael Gough, Diana Dors, Ty Hardin and Judy Geeson have all perished by this time.

Although numerous sections of *Berserk!* consist of documentary footage of the performers and animals of Billy Smart's Circus, this isn't really a film about circus life. Rather, it's about the expendability of show-people. Early on in the film, Joan Crawford tells Michael Gough that everybody is expendable. Later, she tells a group of talent agents not to waste her time with 'broken-down has-beens', stating that she's looking for something 'fresh', what she calls 'a new face with an exciting act', adding that she doesn't want an old-timer with wrinkles. The irony of this statement could not have been lost, either on the sixty-year-old actress herself or the audience looking at her. This is just one of many instances in which a character's remark in *Berserk!* seems heavily loaded, providing an ironic commentary on the actor's own career, image and reputation for the amusement of the audience. Yet there's no twinkle in Crawford's eye or tongue in her cheek when Monica tells the agents what she does and doesn't want. On the contrary, she plays it absolutely straight, seemingly rising above any suggestion that she might well be considered an old-timer performing the same familiar act after more than forty years in the film business.

Ernest Mathijs challenges the widespread notion that acting in cult movies is typically hammy, one-dimensional and unsubtle in his essay 'From Being to Acting: Performance in Cult Cinema', regarding such claims as being founded on prejudice (2012: 136). Joan Crawford's acting in *Berserk!* substantiates his argument as she performs with all the conviction, subtlety and complexity of her Oscar-winning role in *Mildred Pierce* (Curtiz 1945). However, exploitation or cult thrillers require much more than conviction, subtlety and complexity from their performers. This is partly due to the low-grade aspects that characterise this genre, including badly lit and composed shots, as well as poorly synched sound. It's also due to the reception of such films, especially in seedy cinemas. Here, excitable and raucous audiences often make their reactions felt noisily with whistles, screams, shouts, gasps and guffaws. This requires performers to adopt an acting style as bold and broad as the other elements of the film's production, marketing and exhibition. Consequently, the actors that typically excel in this genre are those who enjoy playing to the gallery and portraying their characters with broad brushstrokes.

Theatricality and histrionics often lie at the heart of cult cinema, along with loud sound. Frequent screams, bangs, shrieks, crashes, squeals and explosions on the soundtrack have proven to be an effective way of regaining the attention of a lively audience as much as a sudden burst of unnerving silence. An aesthetic of extremes has often been employed in low-budget thrillers, one that is sometimes so pervasive that an actor's performance needs both to compete with it and blend in seamlessly to avoid seeming incongruous. Actors also need to avoid being judged as naïve or incompetent on the grounds that they seem ignorant of the conventions of this genre; notably that cult films are meant to be fantasy not reality, worthless not worthy, clichéd not original, and trash not art.

Dors' sensational referential performances

For aficionados of trashy cult thrillers, *Berserk!*'s finest moments may well include Diana Dors' death scene. The actress is certainly at her most spectacular here, wearing a pink, purple and black basque as her stage outfit, one that exposes her long legs and ample bosom. After Crawford's Monica has announced to a capacity audience that Lazlo will saw a woman in half, the magician introduces Matilda as his beautiful and brave assistant. Dors then makes her appearance from behind a set of curtains with a beaming smile. She runs into the ring with a dainty little wiggle, all sweet and feminine and not at all like the tough woman that has been seen so far. Dors camps it up a little at this moment, until Lazlo says that maybe she's too dumb to be frightened or trusts him completely. Then she stands with her hands on her hips in typically Dorsian style, looking round at the audience with a fixed smile on her face and a glare in her eyes, clearly indicating that she's neither dumb nor trusting.

Once secured inside a horizontal box, however, Dors can do no more than wiggle her toes in her high-heeled shoes, shake her blonde hair and bat her long black eyelashes. As a drumroll begins and the lights fade and glow red, the diegetic audience becomes agog with anticipation. Philip Madoc's Lazlo gazes down at Matilda with a slightly psychotic look as the large steel circular saw begins to spin. After the camera has cut to Judy Geeson, Joan Crawford and Ty Hardin watching through the curtain, a close-up of Dors' face reveals Matilda looking anxious and confused, her lips and eyes opening wide. At the point where she starts screaming, the camera pulls in rapidly on her strangely orange face so that her big glossy lips fill the screen. As the saw cuts deep into Matilda's side, the camera is almost swallowed between her lips, emphasising that her big mouth has proven to be her undoing after all. Dors' eyes reopen during her final screen moments, Matilda staring in shock and horror as the saw slices through her waist and spine to disconnect her torso from her hips.

Dors' death scene is not only spectacular and ironic but also more theatrical than realistic. Rather than terrifying or challenging to watch, it's thoroughly absorbing and amusing. Yet, although it's one of the film's highlights, it wasn't actually original since Dors had previously been cut in two by a deranged young man with a circular saw on American television in 1961 during an episode of *Alfred Hitchcock Presents* called 'The Sorcerer's Apprentice' (see Cale 2021: 107). When projected onto the big screen in colour, however, Dors' bisection made a greater impression. It was certainly much larger than life in *Berserk!* as well as a lot more garish. In addition to having a more sensational impact, Dors' death scene here can be seen as typically 'cult movie-ish' in that the performance is based on an earlier one. As such, it conforms to what Ernest Mathijs calls 'referential' acting, which he argues is prevalent in cult movies and defines as 'the self-conscious design of a performance on the basis of a previous one, often by the same actor, but also based on real-life templates, exemplary models or clichéd stereotypes, including homage, quotes, plagiarisms and allusions' (2012: 141). Interestingly, he notes that this 'has affinities with the presentational character of a magician's stage show, being rife with winks, nudges and signature gestures (and even direct address)' (141).

As a magician's assistant, it seems natural for Matilda to be self-consciously performative when entering the circus ring. Yet she might also be expected to keep up the act of sweetness and charm when the magician announces that she's either too dumb to be frightened or trusts him completely. Here, for instance, she might smile, bat her eyelashes, blush, bow her head or even blow Lazlo a kiss. Consequently, when Dors reacts by standing with her hands on her hips and looking round with a steely glare in her eyes, she seems to be addressing a non-diegetic cinema audience, one fully aware that she's a tough character with very little faith in her husband or anyone else. At this point, the use of a signature gesture directly addressed to the film spectator exemplifies Mathijs' definition of referential acting.

This is not the only time in *Berserk!* that Dors cites her own previous performances. Indeed, she does so during one of her biggest scenes, played opposite Ty Hardin. After entering Frank Hawkins' caravan uninvited and discovering the hunky tightrope walker stripped to the waist, she saunters suggestively towards him, swinging her hips from side to side, highlighting the fact that – first and foremost – she's Swingin' Dors. Although Frank makes it clear that Matilda's sexual advances are unwelcome, she settles herself onto his leather sofa and refuses to go away. Here, the actress adopts a playful tone but also speaks in an arch sort of way to sound knowingly naïve. She's all big eyes and smiles too, while exhibiting her long shapely legs. Once Hardin has joined her on the couch, Dors pulls him towards her, licking her lips lasciviously before pressing her torso against his bare flesh. As every gesture is slightly overdone, these actions imply that Matilda is feigning sexual interest in Frank and that her real objective is to steal him away from Monica.

While this seems like a credible reading, the other way to account for Dors' subtle overplaying of this seduction scene is to ascribe it to a self-conscious citation of a performance once produced when she was regarded as one of the world's most successful sex symbols. This certainly seems to be the case when Dors places her hands upon Hardin's shoulders as the seduction scene unfolds. While pressing herself against her co-actor's bare chest, Dors' left hand finds its way to the back of his neck. For a moment, her right hand strokes his collarbone but then, as they kiss, it crawls up Hardin's neck to a position by his ear, recalling a gesture that she used with Tom Tryon in 1956. As can be seen in Figure 7.1, the actress's fingers remain splayed out at this point with her long pink fingernails shining, assuming the archetypal persona of the spiderwoman.

Yet this isn't just an evocation of the femmes fatales of 1940s film noir but, more specifically, Dors' own performance ten years earlier in *The Unholy Wife* (Farrow 1957). Now, however, the honeyed vocal tones, provocative pout, spidery fingers and other visible assets that once beguiled Tryon's character San Sanders have evidently lost their seductive power. Although Matilda tries everything – including rubbing her hand over Hardin's bare shoulder in a circular motion, gently caressing his earlobe and softly brushing his cheek with her thumb – Frank firmly pushes her away, eventually removing her bodily from his caravan and throwing her down in the dirt outside to the amusement of passers-by.

Figure 7.1 A screenshot of Matilda (Dors) as she attempts to seduce Frank (Ty Hardin) in *Berserk!*, recalling a similar scene with Tom Tryon in *The Unholy Wife* (1957). (YouTube, last accessed 17/02/2021.)

The citation of a performance from her Hollywood star vehicle during her seduction scene in *Berserk!* not only corresponds to Mathijs' definition of 'referential acting' in cult cinema but also constitutes what might be called 'has-been acting'. This, I would argue, is best understood as an attempt by an actor to affirm what she or he once was by citing something that they did at the height of their stardom. Dors' references to performances produced at her peak as an international movie star are indicative of 'has-been acting', establishing her as a post-peak star actor in 1966. These recall the height of her stardom and acknowledge how much it has faded during the intervening period. A more forceful reminder of Dors' own fall from grace could hardly be imagined than the humiliating spectacle of Matilda being roughly expelled from a caravan and cast down into the dirt.

Salvage

While Diana Dors adopted the referential acting technique of cult cinema and performed as a 'has-been' in *Berserk!*, Joan Crawford maintained the style of performance here that won her an Oscar for her title role in *Mildred Pierce* twenty years earlier. By ignoring the nonsensical aspects of *Berserk!*'s cliché-ridden plot and its mediocre dialogue, the legendary Hollywood star maintained a magnificently stellar appearance and performance. Evidently, Herman Cohen and Jim O'Connolly were not committed to making this a full-blown schlocky horror despite its exclamatory title suggesting someone or something being out of control. Although the scenario consisted of a series of implausible murders by an improbable killer, the overall tone of the film remained tame, enabling the majority of the cast to follow Crawford's lead and perform with a high degree of seriousness and conviction. This restricted opportunities for self-reflexivity, as well as excessive or extreme reactions. Nevertheless, Diana Dors proved to be the exception when adopting a degree of self-mockery. Having said that, what she didn't do was send herself up (or send up her former self) with an elaborate or exaggerated parody, which would have jarred uncomfortably with Crawford's performance. Dors' self-mockery remained subtle, restricted largely to the twinkle in her eye that lets the audience in on the joke.

Diana Dors might well be pitied for her role as the loud-mouthed magician's assistant Matilda, especially when she's presented as an over-the-hill sex symbol who can no longer seduce men in the way her characters did ten years earlier. Nevertheless, many cult movie aficionados are likely to applaud the actress for the way she gamely forsakes personal dignity in *Berserk!*. Dors certainly exhibits an awareness of the peculiar demands of exploitation cinema when performing in this movie. She seems to understand that this type of film required her not only to repeatedly humiliate herself but also to broaden her acting while playing with her tongue in her cheek or with a knowing twinkle in her eye. In doing so, she plays an active role in poking fun at Matilda. This enables her to take some credit for the laughter provoked among audiences when her attempted seduction fails and she's manhandled out of Frank's caravan and thrown down into an undignified heap on the ground or when she's tricked into being sawn in half. What salvages Dors' reputation here is that she's not only willing to be presented in such situations but also seems to relish the chance to pastiche her own previous screen performances. One thing that it definitely affirms is that Dors hadn't lost her sense of humour or her ability to laugh at herself in 1966, despite losing almost everything else.

Chapter 8

Popping in and out as a virtuosic guest star in *The Pied Piper* (1972)

Based on the famous Grimm Brothers' folktale of 1816, Jacques Demy's *The Pied Piper* provided a small role for Diana Dors that showcased her virtuosic acting skills. The forty-year-old actress was billed as a 'Guest Star' when playing the Burgermeister's buxom, bossy and bad-tempered wife. She makes a big impression here as Frau Poppendick in some highly theatrical costumes, the actress deftly conveying her character's marital and maternal failings in just six short scenes. Although depicting her as an archetypal fairy-tale villainess, she draws heavily upon her own public image and screen persona, which was necessary given the brevity and scarcity of her scenes. This provides an opportunity to consider what well-known stars do with small character parts and how such seemingly incidental roles give them a chance to flex their acting muscles while exploiting their celebrity.

A children's tale for adults

The Pied Piper was an international collaboration between the UK-based Goodtimes Enterprises and the American-owned Sagittarius Productions that was shot on location in Bavaria and at studios in London. This ambitious project involved one of France's leading filmmakers directing a large cast of British and European actors with an internationally famous Scottish folk singer in the title role. After releasing several chart-topping albums in the 1960s – including *Sunshine Superman* (1966), *Mellow Yellow* (1967) and *The Hurdy Gurdy Man* (1968) – Donovan promised to draw a sizable music-loving crowd to see him play Hamelin's famous piper. Meanwhile, director Jacques Demy seemingly guaranteed that international film critics and art-house audiences would also flock to see his unique interpretation of this well-known fable.

On paper, Demy was the perfect candidate to create a whimsical musical folktale, one that could delight adults as much as children. After being nominated for an Oscar for his screenplay for *Les Parapluies de Cherbourg/The Umbrellas of Cherbourg* (1964), the French filmmaker enjoyed critical and commercial success across Europe and the USA, especially for *Les Demoiselles de Rochefort/The Young Girls of Rochefort* (1967). Yet Demy was also known to be artistically uncompromising, which proved disastrous when *Model Shop* (1969) was made at Columbia Pictures in Hollywood. His incest-themed *Peau d'Âne/Donkey Skin* (1970) proved unpalatable for many moviegoers, particularly those who found it too kitsch and gaudy to be taken seriously. Demy subsequently darkened his palette for *The Pied Piper* to create a grim depiction of social inequity and peasant persecution, sexual bartering and marital misery, religious corruption and rodent infestation in the middle ages. This was to be no flight into fantasy but rather a children's story full of adult themes.

Any attempt to transform this Brothers Grimm tale of Hamelin's mysterious rat-catcher into a heartwarming scenario for the enjoyment of family audiences around the world was thoroughly rejected, resulting in something altogether macabre and disconcerting. As Anne Duggan writes in her study of Demy's fairy-tale films *Queer Enchantments*, the director used 'black humor to caricature in less than subtle ways the socio-political and religious authorities of Hamelin' to produce a 'very modern allegory about the blind obedience to power that results not only in exploitation of the people ... but also and quite significantly in mass destruction' (Duggan 2013: 72).

Upon seeing a rough cut, Andrew Birkin – who had co-written the screenplay with Mark Peploe – tried to dissociate from it (Yule 1988: 66). Meanwhile, co-producer David Puttnam later described the film as 'a piece of shit', regretting that his admiration for Demy had prevented him from intervening to rein in the director's excesses to make it more marketable (1988: 66–7). Released with an 'A' certificate into British cinemas for Christmas 1972, it was deemed unsuitable for under eight-year-olds, with adult supervision being recommended. The sight of burning human bodies during the opening shots was enough to shock many young viewers and horrify their parents. An astonishing allegory, this reworking of the popular folk story baffled critics and audiences alike, resulting in scathing reviews and poor box-office returns, although it did eventually receive a standing ovation when screened at the Festival de Paris in November 1975 (Duggan 2013: 71).

Popping in and out

Diana Dors' six brief scenes in *The Pied Piper* are all contained within the first 30 minutes as Frau Poppendick plans her daughter Lisa's wedding to the Baron's son Franz, overseeing preparations for the banquet and the making of the wedding dress, as well as taking part in the ceremony. Despite limited screen time, the star cuts a striking figure, largely due to her extraordinary costumes. As the story is set in Germany in 1349, she's elaborately dressed in pseudo-medieval clothing. When first appearing on screen, for instance, she wears a red robe with a towering white wimple-like headpiece. Yet, despite the large crucifix hanging about her neck, a cleavage-exposing neckline makes her look more like a prostitute than a nun. This impression is further highlighted when she's seated at a kitchen table with her skirts raised to her thighs and her feet in a tub of water. As she delivers her one line of dialogue here, Dors' slurred speech indicates that Frau Poppendick is inebriated.

This woman's wanton nature is confirmed when Dors makes her second appearance 5 minutes later in a short scene with John Hurt as Franz, who seizes her in an amorous embrace. As they hold their bodies tightly together, Frau Poppendick pouts and bats her eyelashes at the young nobleman who is betrothed to her daughter Lisa. After his departure, she turns to a young maidservant and declares, 'And what are you staring at, you idle fool?' with her hands on hips in classic Dorsian style. In just under twenty seconds, this scene establishes that the intemperate hausfrau is an unfaithful wife and a bad mother, as well as being shamelessly brazen and bad tempered.

It becomes patently obvious 10 minutes later that the debauched female head of the Poppendick household is prostituting her pubescent daughter by marrying her off to Hamelin's most eligible bachelor, with whom she herself is having an affair. While vigorously chopping meat in her kitchen, she issues instructions to the chef about the forthcoming wedding banquet and to the seamstress about her daughter's wedding dress. As she orders the servants about, Frau Poppendick marches back and forth wearing a bloodstained white apron while brandishing a long knife before her crotch, emphasising its phallic significance and her castrating nature. Her insistence that the frail and anemic-looking bride-to-be needs to be given more of a bust enables the actress to showcase her own curvaceous figure while betraying the extent to which her character is prepared to sacrifice her daughter's sexual innocence for her own social ambitions.

Apart from a very brief scene in which Lisa bumps into her mother when fleeing from some rats in the garden, Dors does not appear again until the wedding day. When she descends a staircase into the kitchen alongside her daughter, Frau Poppendick once again commands attention. On this occasion, she wears a long-flowing wine-red velvet gown with elaborate green silk sleeves and a remarkable headpiece reminiscent of large cattle horns (as can be seen in Figure 8.1). Of all the bizarre outfits that Evangeline Harrison created for *The Pied Piper*, this one was the most extraordinary.

Having previously designed costumes for Roger Corman's *De Sade* (1969) and Roman Polanski's *Macbeth* (1971), Harrison was well versed in the creation of highly symbolic, theatrical and spectacular clothes. For Frau Poppendick's wedding outfit, she designed something truly astonishing involving a headpiece that accentuated her bovine qualities, rendering her half-woman and half cow. Yet, while the wicked woman has no problem with her pseudo-horns, she finds everything else to be wrong with her wedding garb, including the colours, the sleeves and the pleats. 'God, what a mess!', she declares blasphemously, clearly anxious that she won't be able to make a good impression at the ceremony. However, once the family set foot outside to join the procession to the steps of the half-built cathedral, she assumes a stately air of dignity and decorum. Conscious of the bystanders' admiring stares, she raises her face and adopts a smug superiority while piously clasping her hands before her. In this way, she processes through the street to the accompanying sound of church bells, at last a seemingly happy hypocrite.

This paves the way for Dors' final scene, the much-anticipated wedding banquet. Here, Frau Poppendick sits at the top table with the bishop (Peter Vaughan) on her right and the groom (John Hurt) on her left. As can be seen in the image below, the young bride sits next to her new husband with a glum and vacant expression, seemingly lost

Figure 8.1 A screen shot of Diana Dors when guest starring in Jacques Demy's *The Pied Piper* (1972) as Frau Poppendick in her bovine headdress alongside John Hurt, as her lover and new son-in-law, and Cathryn Harrison as the neglected daughter and unloved bride. (YouTube, last accessed 21/02/2021.)

in her own private thoughts, while her mother laughs flirtatiously with her son-in-law, conveying a strong sense that they are still romantically involved with each other. Dors has just one line in this scene ('Oh yes, let's have some cake!'), which she exclaims in a high-pitched voice while clapping her hands. At her command, the large wedding cake is brought forth. Yet this intricate replica of the cathedral soon elicits shock rather than delight from the assembled company when revealed to be full of rats. Dors is the first to scream at the sight of them, jumping up from her place at the table and clasping John Hurt, who she clings to as the rats scamper about the room and the guests flee. Finally, Dors is seen in the background making her departure from the room, scene and film, never to be heard of again.

Apart from her spectacular costumes, what's striking about Dors' performance in all six of these scenes is that it's much more animated and altogether broader than her previous roles, even that of Matilda in *Berserk!* (1967). She performs Frau Poppendick as comedic and, although it isn't quite pantomimic, it's certainly histrionic with an exaggerated set of physical gestures and facial expressions. Her words are mostly accompanied by emphatic actions, adding weight to her few short lines of dialogue while drawing attention to her presence in the shot. This could suggest that the actress adopted a less nuanced style of performance to communicate with a young audience, believing this to be a children's film.

Yet, this would require her to ignore the film's morbid aspects and sexual themes, which make it inappropriate for youngsters.

It's more likely that Dors' emphatic and histrionic performance in *The Pied Piper* was influenced by Evangeline Harrison's gaudy theatrical costumes. These vibrant outfits not only heighten the unholy, animalistic and exhibitionist persona of Frau Poppendick but also lend her an appearance that is culturally associated with both mediaeval history and folkloric fantasy. They even turn her into an archetypal pantomime dame, a role conventionally performed on stage by a middle-aged man. Yet these costumes also impose certain restrictions upon Dors. Firstly, the elaborate headdresses not only constantly conceal her trademark blonde hair but also frequently obscure her face. Given the likelihood that some of her facial expressions will be missed, the actress appears to compensate with her body. This would certainly account for her broader physical gesticulations here. Interestingly, where Dors' tightly fitted costumes – notably, her corsets and basques – restricted the fluidity and flexibility of her body in the 1950s, Harrison's loosely fitted costumes enabled her not only to breathe more deeply but also to move more freely. As a result, she moves constantly, her body rippling, quivering, swaying and undulating. While motivated by Frau Poppendick's nervous anxiety about the wedding, Dors' incessant movements seem to result from something else; namely, the need to attract the audience's attention.

Movement is inherently eye-catching and so many character actors maximise their small roles in films by moving about, typically using their whole body to execute elaborate gestures in long shots. Dors not only does this in *The Pied Piper* but also employs other methods commonly associated with character acting, displaying what Ernest Mathijs calls 'vivid expressiveness', as previously discussed in Chapter 5 (2012: 143). This is particularly noticeable in the wedding banquet scene, where the guest star risks being lost among a crowd of actors in some equally extraordinary costumes. During her last few seconds on screen, she appears to make a concerted effort to be noticed. Consequently, when responding to the suggestion that they have cake, she produces a squeal of delight before declaring 'Oh yes . . .!' Having completed the line with the words 'let's have some cake!' to the accompaniment of clapping hands, Dors executes an elaborate gesture that involves holding her hands together and tilting them swiftly downwards in a ringing action.

Part of the problem for Dors here though is the constantly moving camera, which further reduces her limited screen time. Moreover, she's mostly seen seated to the left of John Hurt, who tends to hog the 'star slot' more than any other actor (as seen in Figure 8.1). It's from this more marginal position that Dors performs her squeal, clap and hand-ringing routine. Yet the latter is almost lost when the camera pans to the right. Everything here seems to be conspiring against the actress. Fortunately, however, it results in an effective performance since – while some of the nuances of the actress's acting may be lost – the star's attention-seeking behaviour overall adds to the character's desperation. Consequently, while Frau Poppendick's big day turns out to be a disaster, Dors' succeeds in making a spectacular exit. This ensures that her performance remains memorable even though her character is entirely forgotten about by everyone in Hamelin after the rat-infested cake has created chaos. It also presented the forty-year-old Dors as a highly competent character actress.

Behaving like a perfect guest star

The year before Diana Dors was hired to play a character part in *The Pied Piper*, she had received rave reviews for her performance on stage in *Three Months Gone*, first at the Royal Court and then at Duchess Theatre in London's West End (as discussed in Chapter 4). Consequently, she took on the role of Frau Poppendick as a critically acclaimed stage actor and commercially successful theatre star. When billing her as a 'Guest Star' in the film's credit sequence, the producers David Puttnam and Sandy Lieberson gave Dors the smallest kind of starring role in a movie, one that implied that the role she was playing was smaller than might be expected for someone with such a high profile. While brief and largely contained within the first quarter of the movie, Dors' appearances in *The Pied Piper* promised to provide moviegoers around the world with a glimpse of her recently celebrated acting skills. This may account, in part at least, for her actorly performance here. After all, both her appearance and performance as Frau Poppendick are essentially theatrical. Indeed, everything about her suggests that she's consciously presenting to an audience, performing as though in a play, pageant or pantomime.

An attempt to capitalise on the star's reputation as a stage actor could well have motivated such a bravura performance, one characterised by vivid expressivity, perpetual movement and bold physical gestures. Yet this could just as easily have resulted from Dors' perception of her character as an archetypal villainess of folklore, fairy tales and Christmas pantomimes. Consequently, Frau Poppendick is not so much a depiction of middle-class medieval German matrons than the most grotesque archetype of European folk and fairy tales: namely, the wicked stepmother who persecutes the young hero and/or heroine but eventually gets her comeuppance at the end when her evil plan is thwarted and justice restored. As a mythical rather than historical character, Dors has licence to dispense with naturalism and overact.

It would also seem that Dors had the freedom to replace naturalism with theatricality as a guest star, especially if the rules that typically apply to the rest of the cast don't necessarily apply to this type of performer. Being a guest star in a film presumably involves performing a character that doesn't quite belong to the diegetic world, a sort of temporary inhabitant who appears briefly before vanishing. If this character only partially participates in the dramatic scenario, they necessarily remain semi-detached, almost belonging to some other realm. The guest star is certainly not as embedded as other actors, particularly when only featuring in a segment of the film.

Leading actors, on the other hand, appear in scene after scene in the guise of their character, so that after a while audiences come to see and hear the characters being played more than the stars playing them. Typically, star identities become obscured and subsumed within fictional characters as a film's narrative develops, so it's likely that they have fully become their character in the minds of the audience by the final scene. Guest stars, meanwhile, have insufficient time for this transformation to occur, so that their own identities are retained to a much greater extent when making their exit. In other words, the character they are playing (say, Frau Poppendick) has insufficient time for their persona to become independent from that of the star (Diana Dors).

Being largely bound to the star's own distinctive persona, a character performed by a guest star is similar to one played by a celebrity in a 'cameo role'. Cameos ordinarily offer well-known people the chance to be themselves on screen when making a small and inconsequential appearance in a movie, one that's basically intended to reward the careful attention of audiences. Ernest Mathijs writes in 'From Being to Acting' that, 'a cameo act is a short appearance by a publicly known person who is instantly recognizable – and therefore harder to accept as a character than as him or herself' (2012: 144). However, cameos come in all shapes and sizes, having various functions and effects.

People originally made cameo appearances in films as 'non-descript' extras within a scene, appearing as themselves rather than as fictional characters, such as the director Alfred Hitchcock in his own films (Mathijs 2012: 144). Over time, however, cameo roles have taken on aspects of characterisation and performance, even incorporating the delivery of lines of dialogue and the adornment of historical costumes, wigs and prosthetics that disguise rather than disclose the real identity of the performer. This includes the appearance of rock star Keith Richards delivering several lines to Johnny Depp in *Pirates of the Caribbean: At World's End* (Verbinski 2007), as described by Mathijs (2012: 144).

There's actually a long tradition of well-known actors making cameo appearances in popular British films, including Alastair Sim as a impecunious film producer in *Lady Godiva Rides Again* (Launder 1951), Margaret Rutherford as an eccentric pet-store owner in *An Alligator Named Daisy* (Lee Thompson 1955) and Diana Dors' as a Dr Kildare-obsessed housewife buying fish at Billingsgate Market in *The Sandwich Man* (Hartford-Davis 1965). In all these cases, a well-known actor plays a fictional character within just one scene of a film, one that can be easily removed without undermining the continuity of the narrative or overall significance of the plot.

Like many other British movie actors, Diana Dors performed numerous cameos, including in *It's Not Cricket* (Rich 1949), *The Saint's Return* (Friedman 1953) and *Allez France!* (Dhéry 1964). However, these were all much smaller roles than the one she performs in *The Pied Piper* and none of them were given character names in the credits. In contrast, Frau Poppendick is a more developed character with a distinct identity and a crucial narrative function as both the organiser of the wedding and the primary representative of child-abusing townsfolk. She also appears in too many scenes for this to be a genuine cameo role. Nevertheless, Dors' role in *The Pied Piper* still has cameo-like qualities that enable the star to shine through despite using a performance style that's associated with character acting (namely, vivid expressivity). This produces a hybrid performance that seems appropriate for what is effectively a star-character part; that is, a character part played by a star.

Dors acquired a prominent yet ambivalent status within *The Pied Piper*'s hierarchy of performers as the film's one and only guest star. Although apparently less important than the actual stars of the film (those billed above the title; namely, Donovan and Jack Wild), she's considerably more significant than the character actors in small roles, such as Sammie Winmill as the seamstress Gretel and David Nettheim as the chef Kulik. Dors' celebrity made it impossible for her to slip seamlessly into her screen role in the way that the relatively unknown Winmill and Nettheim do. While they can fully inhabit their small roles from the instant they appear on screen, Dors still hasn't become fully subsumed by Frau Poppendick even at the end of her sixth and final scene. This fact disqualifies her from being categorised as a 'character actor' here even though her performance bears so many features associated with character acting.

Bravura

Diana Dors' acting in *The Pied Piper* displays a great deal of technical skill and brilliance, the very essence of virtuosity. While asserting her credentials as an accomplished actor, this suggested confidence in her abilities given that it could so easily be condemned as either bad or ham acting. When performances fail to be convincing, realistic and/or invisible, they are usually written off as incompetent or amateurish. Dors' performance as Frau Poppendick could well be deemed 'over-acting', implying that she misjudged the degree of ostentation required here. If so, she would indeed be called a 'Ham', which conventionally denotes an actor who becomes overly theatrical when trying too hard to draw attention to him or herself.

To walk the fine line between great and ham acting takes both courage and skill. It's certainly not for the faint-hearted or performers with a limited range. To be truly effective, the virtuoso needs to display equal amounts of finesse and histrionic power. Diana Dors displays both in *The Pied Piper*, having the confidence to act like a *virtuosa* at the peak of her skills as a performer, while continuing to use her trademark gestures, poses and expressions. In so doing, she demonstrates how commanding stars can be in character parts. And, while she makes a significant contribution to Demy's original and artful rendition of this well-known tale, *The Pied Piper* contributes something both distinctive and bizarre to her film portfolio.

Chapter 9

Perfect when poised in *Steaming* (1985)

Diana Dors shared her final film with the esteemed director Joseph Losey, who made his reputation as a film director in Britain in the 1960s after escaping the McCarthy anti-Communist trials. His collaborations with playwright Harold Pinter received considerable praise, notably his BAFTA award-winning *The Servant* (1963), Golden Globe-nominated *Accident* (1967) and *The Go-Between* (1971), which won the Palme d'Or at the Cannes Film Festival, along with four BAFTA awards. Consequently, the American director enjoyed his greatest success as a filmmaker during the period when Dors' film career was in the doldrums. In the early to mid 1970s, as the actress regained a foothold in the British film industry with small roles in horror films and sex comedies, Losey directed some of the world's top female stars, including Jane Fonda in *A Doll's House* (1973) and Glenda Jackson in *The Romantic Englishwoman* (1975). In 1984, however, the highly acclaimed director and under-rated film actress came together to make *Steaming* (1985), based on the award-winning stage play by Nell Dunn.

Dunn came to prominence with her short story collections *Up the Junction* (1963) and *Poor Cow* (1967), notably when these were adapted for the screen by Ken Loach in the late sixties. Celebrated as a chronicler of working-class women's lives, her work came from the heart and a great deal of lived experience. Using a realist style, she combined an uncompromising frankness, a non-judgmental approach to her character's failings, a forthright feminism and a mix of strong language with more lyrical soliloquys. *Steaming* won the Laurence Olivier Award for Best New Comedy when staged at the Theatre Royal in London's Stratford East in

1981. When this was adapted for the big screen, Dunn collaborated with Losey's wife Patricia on the screenplay to preserve the spirit of the play.

Cast in a pivotal role, Diana Dors produced a performance for Losey that involved glamour and gravitas in equal measure, utilising her famous star image, trademark gestures and understated naturalism with a great deal of poise. From the opening to the closing shots, she quietly wove her way through the film, helping to unite a heterogeneous group of women played by very different kinds of actress. In this chapter, I shall investigate how Dors was able to utilise her glamorous star image, reveal her strengths as an actor and draw directly on a lifetime's experience as a woman in her curiously central yet peripheral role.

At the centre and the sidelines

Steaming is a dramatic comedy with a multi-generational all-female cast. It's not only feminist but also contentious, angry, funny and heartwarming. Diana Dors plays Violet, the manageress of a municipal baths in London's East End due to be closed down to make way for a leisure centre and car park. The other major cast members include Patti Love as the outspoken, uneducated and highly sexed Josie; Vanessa Redgrave as the demure Nancy, a recently deserted middle-class housewife and mother, and Sarah Miles as the independent and extrovert former jetsetter Sarah, now a successful lawyer whose biological clock is causing her to panic as she ages beyond child-bearing years. In smaller supporting roles are Brenda Bruce as the elderly ailing and anxious Mrs Meadows; Felicity Dean as her daughter Dawn, and Sally Sagoe as a black attendant called Celia. Together, these women work through their differences, difficulties and conflicts to form an invincible united front against the local council and its entrepreneurial ambitions.

Female comradeship lies at the heart of this scenario and, while Patti Love's Josie undergoes the greatest transformation and has the most dramatic speeches, Diana Dors' Violet is the force that unites them all. She's the very image of serenity, sympathy, experience and wisdom, functioning as an agony aunt. As such, she helps some very different women both to unite and be themselves, providing a space in which they can safely bare all – their bodies, frustrations and anxieties.

A happily married mother of four, Violet is as open-minded as she is open-hearted, a working woman who has brought up her children and retained the love of her husband while managing the baths for the last eighteen years. A pragmatic, diligent and caring person, she gets on with everyone while going about her business with a minimum of fuss. Indeed, she would be little more than a background figure if she didn't have such a spectacularly noticeable image. As embodied by the glamorous Diana Dors, Violet invariably stands out, even when half of those around her are naked. While she first appears on screen in a black swimming costume, Dors remains fully clothed throughout the rest of the film, unlike many of her co-stars (notably Patti Love and Sarah Miles) who had to set aside any inhibitions and place their trust in the filmmakers not to exploit their bodies for the mere gratification of male voyeurs.

If men came to see *Steaming* to feast their eyes on the bare breasts, nipples and vaginas that appear fairly regularly, they would have been confronted by the unusual sight of women articulating their own desires, their demands for sexual satisfaction as well as equal rights, economic independence, liberty and respect. For this is primarily a film for women, one that vents female frustration about sexual inequality while also providing an opportunity for women of all ages and social backgrounds to look at and listen to other women. The shabby 19th century Turkish baths (in which the whole of *Steaming* is set) is a place to cleanse and be reborn under the protecting gaze of Diana Dors' Violet.

Dors received third billing here, after Vanessa Redgrave and Sarah Miles, all three names appearing on the posters above the film's title. This reflected their relative star status in the mid-1980s. When Redgrave accepted producer Paul Mills' offer of the role of Nancy, her star power guaranteed that the film would be distributed around the world (via Columbia Pictures) and reviewed by leading critics. As an Oscar-winning and Golden Globe-winning actress, as well as an internationally celebrated British thespian, she ensured the film's status as a prestige picture. As an ardent activist and long-term campaigner for human rights, Redgrave's participation in *Steaming* also confirmed its status as a radical film. She was undoubtedly drawn to the project because of its commitment to feminism, socialism and campaigning as much as the reputations of the screenwriter and the director.

Redgrave's international public profile and star power not only gave her first billing on the posters but also ensured that her name appeared at the start of the film before any other. However, this didn't translate into her playing the central protagonist of Nell Dunn's drama, for this is Josie, performed by Patti Love in the film version. By 1984, Love's best-known film performance was her supporting role as Carol Benson in the crime thriller *The Long Good Friday* (Mackenzie 1980) in which she calls Bob Hoskin's character a 'bastard'. *Steaming* promised to be her 'break through' vehicle since many of its most dramatic scenes involve Josie, including her furious tirade against Nancy and Sarah about their privileges as educated middle-class women. Josie is both the first client to arrive at the baths and the character that undergoes the greatest transformation, evolving from a mouthy, sexually insatiable and uneducated unemployed woman to become the spokesperson for the campaign to save the baths. From a tragic and downtrodden figure, she becomes humorously optimistic and sexually liberated before developing into a more articulate, mature and responsible person. In the end, it's Josie that secures the future of the baths with her arguments at a public meeting. She not only reveals leadership qualities and skills as a public speaker but also displays further potential to become a local politician or councillor.

While charting Josie's transformation and portraying a variety of intense emotions, Patti Love's characterisation and performance skills are repeatedly showcased in *Steaming*. Yet there's something inherently theatrical about her performance, a histrionic quality that makes her seem larger than life. Indeed, her acting has the vivid expressiveness associated with character acting (Mathijs 2012: 143). This is particularly noticeable in her first scene when Josie arrives at the baths dazed and upset after being physically abused by her boyfriend and confides in Violet as they sit facing each other at a table. For a moment, the two women gaze into each other's eyes without speaking. Love's mouth begins to move as she struggles to speak. Meanwhile, Dors waits, unmoving but not unmoved. When Love finally says, 'He's gone. Taken everything', there's a cut to Dors' face looking concerned but also resigned, as though she's not really surprised. This suggests a degree of sympathy for Josie but not an excessive one. Remarkably (as can be seen in Figure 9.1), Violet doesn't seem angry or shocked by the sight of the battered woman, indicating perhaps that this has happened before.

There's something extraordinary about this image, which derives in part from the fact that the actress is so heavily made-up, her lower lip shining with glossy lipstick, the famous dagger eyebrows being finely drawn and her eyelashes heavily coated with black mascara. Despite a thick layer of foundation and the blusher that highlights her cheeks, the face is careworn with heavy bags beneath the eyes. Dors looks tired here, drawn and worn out. Yet the hair is thick and shiny, sweeping over her

Figure 9.1 The first close shot of Diana Dors in *Steaming* (Losey 1985) in which Violet gazes at a battered Josie with sympathy rather than anger or shock. (YouTube, last accessed 07/03/2021.)

forehead in a graceful curve like a roller on the Atlantic Ocean, cascading down onto her shoulders in silvery white waves. Beautifully styled and heavily lacquered by Joan Carpenter (who had been hairdressing for movies since 1949), this hairdo proclaimed that Diana Dors was as glamorous as she had been at the height of her stardom in the mid-fifties despite the ravages of time, age and cancer.

While the heavy makeup and stylish hair may distract the audience, something more profound and compelling is conveyed by Dors' eyes, which seem to indicate an understanding of physical and sexual abuse. Rather that stress Violet's sympathetic concern for Josie in this close shot, Dors concentrates instead on producing a knowing look with a gentle tensing of her brow and a slightly unfocused gaze. Her eyes seem to say it all here, implying that she knows all about domestic violence. There's no fuss, however: no making a big scene out of this but rather a calm, reassuring stoicism. Dors presents Violet here as a woman of experience but also as a non-judgmental 'shoulder to cry on' and a 'pillar of strength'.

When Josie asks how her man could have walked out like that, a reverse-shot reveals Love's tear-stained and apparently bruised face. This is a thin unlined face with wide eyes, framed by a thick mane of dark brown curls. There appears to be a large purple bruise at the left-hand side of her mouth and a deep gash through her lower lip. It makes for a striking contrast with Dors' face and is the very image of incomprehension, vulnerability and defeat. Love's eyes drop in shame as Josie admits to Violet that her boyfriend called her a 'slag' before leaving. After describing how he went mad when she called him a 'German puff', for which she received the blow to her mouth, Love falls onto her knees. Dors remains still, her gaze unwavering as Love touches her battered lip with her fingertips and gazes up to the ceiling like some victimised heroine in a 19th-century stage melodrama that has been falsely accused and punished by a dastardly villain.

At this point, Dors puts her hand on Love's shoulder and squeezes it gently before saying, 'Why don't you have a good stream, darling?'. After placing her own hand on her co-actor's knee, Love lowers her head onto it like a little child, allowing Dors to run her fingers through the dark curls, caressing them as Josie speaks of needing to get a job and stand on her own two feet. Yet she quickly becomes desperate, seeming almost mad when she declares in an emphatic whisper that she has to have excitement or she'll die. At this point, Love looks up into the face of a woman who knows all about standing on her own two feet, earning her own living and living a life that is anything but boring, one who also knows about the price to be paid for such things.

The gravitas of Dors' performance here comes from age and experience but also from being able to simply be herself and let her character's thoughts and feelings shine through in the look of her eyes rather than elaborate hand gestures or facial expressions. The star doesn't try too hard to bring her character to life, making no attempt whatsoever to compete with her co-actor for the camera or the audience's attention. She has several close-shots in this poignant scene with which to convey her character's reactions, even if Love has most of the dialogue and a much greater range of emotions to perform. Dors is present, attentive and engaged throughout it all. She seems to have very little (if any) concern to let the audience know that she's giving a performance in the way that Love is doing. Indeed, her performance in *Steaming* resembles her acting in *Is Your Honeymoon Really Necessary?*, which she made back in 1953 when, as a glamorous twenty-one-year-old starlet, she was more concerned to demonstrate that she could act like star than a character actor (see Chapter 5).

Dors performs with a quiet poise and a strong sense of self-possession in *Honeymoon* and *Steaming*, using small naturalistic gestures rather than bold or emphatic ones, while putting as much of herself into her role as possible. Consequently, her characters Candy and Violet are – to all intents and purposes – versions of Diana Dors, relying heavily on her screen persona to render them interesting, engaging, credible and lifelike. Yet in *Steaming*'s opening scene, audiences can see both Diana Dors and her character Violet, the latter slowly emerging the more she speaks. This is particularly noticeable when, in her second close shot of the film, Dors' full glossy lips break into a knowing smile and then, while gently shaking her head, she says, 'Now that it's 'appened, you've just gotta face it.' While the tones of Violet's voice are recognisably Dorsian, the Cockney accent and dropped aitches are not. Consequently, it's in this accent that Violet resides as a character in her own right, as something separate from Diana Dors.

Violet gives way

James Naremore has offered a useful way of untangling the relationship of a film actor and their screen character in *Acting in the Cinema*, one that also recognises the way in which a vivid star image can obscure an actor's craft. His discussion of Cary Grant is especially instructive in this respect, particularly the observation that the actor's image was so dominant that it 'overshadows the technique that helped to create it' (Naremore 1988: 234). Yet analysis of Alfred Hitchcock's *North by Northwest* (1959) not only reveals how precisely Grant developed and executed his performance but also how he drew upon his original training as a stage acrobat when repeatedly performing the same action in take after take (225). Naremore argues that this training also helped the star to perform 'small actions with absolute clarity', while retaining 'technical control over degrees of expression, so that he could produce a series of distinctly shaded reactions in close-up' (225).

Like Cary Grant, Dors' dominant star image could easily overwhelm any sense of the character she's playing and, in the process, disguise her acting ability to make it appear that she's just effortlessly being herself (see Chapter 5). Yet, as a film star, Dors also drew directly upon her early training, which consisted of modelling, elocution lessons and deportment classes. It's not difficult to see that what she gained most of all from these was poise. Throughout her career, poise lent Dors' characters a high degree of confidence, self-possession, authority and dignity. However indecent her star image became, the actress maintained a dignified posture on screen, so that even her 'tarts' conveyed an impressive degree of grace, composure and self-assurance. In the process, she developed her signature poses, including her hands-on-hips stance. This posture signalled strength, stoicism and determination, one that Dors' characters used when refusing to bend or buckle to someone else's will. It was a form of shorthand that told an audience instantly what Dors' character was like and what she was thinking and feeling.

Most actors have certain strengths, something that they are particular good at playing or portraying on screen, which becomes part of their specialism over time and sometimes makes them more effective in one genre rather than another. Naremore, for instance, acknowledges that Cary Grant proved most effective in roles that 'depended on timing, athletic skills and a mastery of small, isolated reactions', which allowed him to thrive in both screwball comedy and action thrillers (225). However, as Naremore also notes, Grant had his limitations as an actor, which included the portrayal of intense emotions or even thoughtful and preoccupied behaviour (225). Similarly, Dors was much better at being resolved, restrained and dignified than pathetic, hysterical or tearful.

When Violet breaks down halfway through *Steaming* after receiving an official letter about the imminent closure of the baths, Dors' performance simply doesn't work. Initially, she conveys distress with a glum face that makes her look more sulky than sad. Dramatically persistent music is added here to inform the audience that something is wrong. When Dors walks slowly towards the camera, Violet appears speechless, too choked with emotion to speak. However, it actually seems more like Dors is struggling to cry than Violet is trying not to, notably when the actress shakes her head despondently while saying that she can't believe it. Her lower lip trembles and her eyes roll in their sockets before she adds, 'They're closing the place down.'

After glancing at the offending piece of paper, she closes her eyes while rubbing her hands together. When explaining that she's just heard the news from the management, she gazes up to the ceiling and then down again at her anxious fingers, gasping for breath. After declaring, 'They're going to close the baths!' in a tearful voice, Dors buries her face in her hands, concealing her tears and saving herself from having to go on conveying distress with her face. Instead, her body pulsates with a succession of small cries. While this display of sorrow seems unconvincing, Dors seems acutely uncomfortable.

The actress is much better at putting on a brave face than a sad one, at demanding respect rather than asking for pity. Consequently, Dors is at her best in *Steaming* when consoling the other women and inspiring them with her serene sympathy and understanding. She's at her absolute best, however, towards the end when she shifts between comedy and pride. Discussing men, Violet laughingly declares, 'They go bald, they go impotent, but they never lose interest in their grub.' Dors' face beams with exactly the same smile here that she used as Mildred in her first film *The Shop at Sly Corner* (King 1946). Her laughter is highly infectious and her comment seems both funny and knowing. Dors deftly segues from sarcasm to sincerity when Violet proceeds to talk about her children, saying, 'If they go out into the world knowing they're loved, it's satisfying. When I look at my kids, I'm proud of them.' The sense of pride seems genuine, as though this is Dors speaking and saying what she truly thinks. It's a small but poignant moment, one that's beautifully offset when Patti Love's Josie declares, 'What a lot of dreamers we are!' to restore the party mood.

During the last moments of her final film, Violet recedes further, allowing Dors to shine through even more clearly. After the women return victorious from the council meeting, she stands with her hands on her hips in one of her classic poses to declare, 'My daughter says that happy endings are old-fashioned.' When Nancy opens a bottle of champagne, they all drink a toast to Violet, although it feels much more like a celebration of Dors' indomitable spirit. Yet, the actress slips out of the limelight to take up a position at the far left of the frame, from which she announces that Josie is the real star of the occasion, having won the battle with the council with her speech. It's almost as though Dors is handing over the baton to the younger actress, especially when Patti Love is positioned close to the centre of the frame. Finally, when the women strip off and jump into the plunge pool for a celebratory dip, Brenda Bruce and Diana Dors (the oldest members of the cast) gaze down upon them from high up on a balcony near the ceiling. If they were in a theatre rather than a public baths, these two actresses would be in the 'gods'.

At the end of *Steaming*, Brenda Bruce looks like an elderly woman with her hair tied up in a scarf and her body covered by a pale blue floral dressing gown. The actress remains in character here as Mrs Meadows. Beside her, Diana Dors creates a very different impression, being so much more glamorous and spectacular. Wearing a short-sleeved black top with long gold chains hanging around her neck, she gazes upwards, her head held high and tilted back, extending her strong neck. Her broad face is wide-eyed and opened-mouthed, a huge smile spread across it. This open face is framed by her platinum blonde hair, which falls luxuriantly onto her shoulders. While the light catches on her cheeks and chin, as well as her pearly white teeth, it mostly illuminates the snowy white hair that has been her trademark for over thirty years. As she looks up, her face is not only full of joy but also wonder, excitement and hope, maybe even relief to have reached this point of cinematic closure, clearly relishing the all-too-rare experience of a happy ending.

Diana Dors is much more than a character called Violet in the final moment of her last film. Every inch a star, she looks glossy and shiny, not quite like the other women here, more image than flesh. If she's not meant to be understood as a real woman, then perhaps she represents the very spirit of the place? Like the municipal baths, she's survived after being considered obsolete. In the end, however, it's clear that she's still needed and has a role to perform in the modern world. She may once have been dismissed as a shabby relic of the past but now she stands proud once again. At the end, *Steaming* leaves audiences with the impression that Diana Dors can be no more eradicated than public baths, the battle of the sexes and even happy endings.

Conclusion
A dubiously Dorsian conclusion

Diana Dors' film career wasn't just disappointing. It was spectacularly unsuccessful.

For all her fame, talent and ambition, she only secured a small number of starring roles, just 8 out of a total of 67 movies between 1946 and 1984. To be specific, Dors received top billing for *Miss Tulip Stays the Night* (1955), *Yield to the Night* (1956), *The Unholy Wife* (1957), *La Ragazza del Palio* (1958) *Tread Softly Stranger* (1958), *Passport to Shame* (1959), *Swedish Wildcats* (1972) and *Keep It Up Downstairs* (1976). None of these won her awards or nominations and most failed miserably at the box-office. Several of them failed on a grand scale in spite of the skilled and celebrated contributors involved in their production, notably *The Unholy Wife* and *La Ragazza del Palio*.

Dors' propensity to fail spectacularly added significantly to the mountain of negative criticism, condemnation and derision already generated by her outspokenness, glitzy image and scandalous behaviour. What she said, how she looked and the things she did generated a stream of sensational tabloid headlines and racy stories in gossip columns. Producers quickly became wary of working with her, while many critics and audiences simply couldn't take her seriously. Yet Dors not only took her work as a film actor very seriously but also consistently created intelligent, nuanced and captivating screen performances for thirty-nine years. From the age of fifteen until her death at fifty-two, she made a significant contribution to all kinds of movies in parts great and small. Her distinctive combination of glamour and intelligence, naturalism and poise, acting skill and self-mockery, provided many films with a memorable moment or two even if the vast majority of them were eminently forgettable and easily dismissed as negligible.

It seems appropriate to reflect on Dors' questionable cinematic achievements and also the possible lasting value of her cinematic work as the end of my study approaches. Even at this late stage, I'm tempted to ask a number of questions. For instance, was the effort Dors put into film acting really worth it given that she attained so little commercial and critical success during her lifetime? Since her major films largely failed to impress critics and attract mass audiences, can there really be any validity in the claim that her big screen performances reward the attention now being given to them by audiences, scholars and both her long-standing and more recently acquired fans? Moreover, is it her starring roles that constitute her greatest accomplishments in cinema or those remarkable moments in which she made a big impression despite limited screen time in what were little more than cameo roles? The following section is intended to tackle this question while bringing the analysis of Dors' acting to a suitable climax.

Diving back in at the deep end

Following a two-year break from filmmaking at the end of the sixties and shortly after giving her critically acclaimed performance as the licentious matriarch Mrs Hanker on the London stage in the hit comedy *Three Months Gone* (see Chapter 4), Dors shot several short scenes in the course of one day for Jerzy Skolimowski. This award-winning Polish film director subsequently incorporated these into the first 15 minutes of his British and West German co-production *Deep End*, which was much admired at the Venice Film Festival in 1970 (Bret 2010: 196). Dors' character (listed in the credits as Mike's 1st Lady Client) makes a big impact near the start of Skolimowski's semi-autobiographical and highly sexualised coming-of-age dramatic comedy (set largely in a London bathhouse), especially when she achieves a self-induced orgasm.

There's no question that *Deep End* belongs to its slim and attractive young leads John Moulder-Brown, as the film's fifteen-year-old protagonist Mike, and Jane Asher, who was nominated for BAFTA's Best Supporting Actress award for her role as Susan. It's Mike and Susan's tortured love affair that dominates the narrative and reaches a bloody climax during the final scene. Yet Dors' astonishing onanistic performance not only provides an eye-opening start to the film but also constitutes one of the most extraordinary movie moments of her career. As her young co-actor writhes against her body, the actress holds him fast by his hair, all the time working her character up to the pinnacle of sexual pleasure by improvising a bizarre and humorous monologue.

Dors' voice, although speaking softly at first, grows stronger as the scene progresses, becoming steadily louder and gruffer to match the increasing force of her actions, which go from gripping Moulder-Brown's jaw to savagely grasping his hair as he desperately squirms in a bid to free himself from her clutches (as can be seen in Figure 10.1). Gasping and panting at this point, Dors' repeated invocation of the footballer George Best's name sounds almost like the braying of a donkey, adding an animalistic quality to her performance.

While delivering her extemporised speech, Dors makes a big play of certain key words, notably 'tackle,' 'dribble' and 'shoot'. These punctuate her character's mantra while imagining the soccer star George Best scoring six goals, particularly the effort to push the football in slowly just

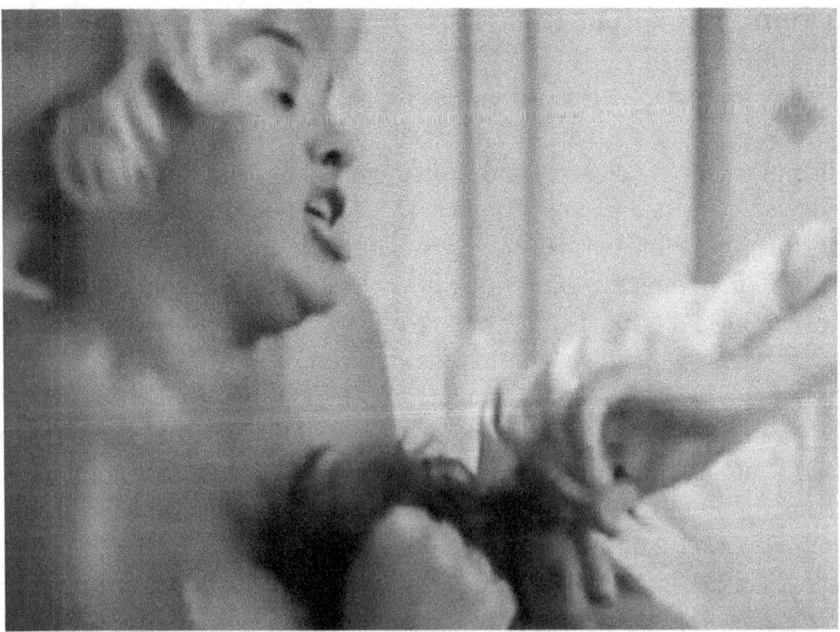

Figure 10.1 A cropped screen shot of Diana Dors reaching a climax as she molests John Moulder-Brown's protagonist in *Deep End* (Skolimowski 1970). (YouTube, last accessed 14/05/2021.)

inside the goalpost, until at last she climaxes while emitting an extended version of his name. At the same time, she throws the astonished woman-handled boy away from her, verbally confirming that she doesn't need him anymore. Suitably sated, Dors and her character disappear from the film; that is, if anyone can forget this astonishing scene in which a mature woman has apparently achieved sexual gratification by forcing herself upon a virginal teenage boy while fantasising about one of the world's most charismatic sporting heroes.

It would seem that Dors' climactic scene in *Deep End* was intended to shock rather than titillate. Her sweaty flesh certainly isn't presented here as an enticing spectacle but rather as something that's both palpably real and grotesquely corporeal. The shiny star who once dazzled and sparkled in her tightly corseted outfits has been transformed into a mass of sweating skin, a figure made of the fleshiest flesh, all plump and slippery but no less strong as she clasps and squeezes her victim ever tighter until she's finally done with him. It's hard to imagine many middle-aged female movie stars allowing themselves to be presented in this way. Yet Dors appears to have had no shame about it. If anything, she seems to relish the opportunity to astonish and disgust, throwing herself into her role with gusto. In so doing, she displays her audacious courage along with her impressive improvisatory acting skills.

As Method actors don't have a monopoly on improvisation, it's not necessary to assume that this scene is an example of Method acting. Indeed, what's particularly striking about it are the dance-like qualities involved when two performers physically grapple with each other's bodies – one holding on and one appearing to try and break free – but all the time moving in rhythm, pulsating synchronously, always in tune with each other and with the guttural, explosive and percussive sounds emanating from Dors' fabulously large throat. If this is a Method performance, however, it's one that corresponds more closely to Sanford Meisner's technique rather than Stella Adler or Lee Strasberg's, which Dors may well have adopted when performing with Tom Tryon during the making of *The Unholy Wife* in 1956, as discussed in Chapter 6.

Watching Dors' orgasm scene in *Deep End* closely for the third or fourth time reveals a highly choreographed routine being played out even if much of it seems spontaneous through an emphasis on reaction rather than action. While both actors are clearly focused on responding to one another, playing off, against and with each other, there's every reason to think that they both knew precisely what the end point would be from the start, ensuring that each and every moment, movement and utterance builds steadily towards the intended and agreed upon goal.

At the start of the seventies, *Deep End* announced to film producers that, despite her success in a starring role on the London stage, Dors was still prepared to take on not only small roles in movies but also shockingly salacious ones. This soon led to her appearance in soft-core pornographic films such as *Swedish Wildcats* (1972) and *What the Swedish Butler Saw* (1975) in addition to smutty sex comedies and horror films (as described in Chapter 4). For many at the time, this wasn't so much an indication that Dors was a fearless or open-minded performer as a desperate and depraved one. She was now generally regarded as a faded film star that was prepared to do anything for money, squandering her talents on shoddy, sleazy productions.

By 1980, it seemed that even Dors herself had decided that it wasn't worth making any more movies after her small role in the sex comedy *Confessions from the David Galaxy Affair* (Roe 1979), devoting her time instead to writing books, such as *For Adults Only* (1978). It was towards the end of this bestselling publication that she admitted that only a handful of the many films she had made were any good, even stating that one of her films had been described in the press as "British film-making 'at its worst'" (Dors 1978: 251). After admitting this, Dors went on to identify J. Lee Thompson's *Yield to the Night* (1956) as one film she could always point to with pride (253). The implication here was that the rest of her movies could be dismissed as worthless. When writing this, Dors placed the lid firmly on such discarded gems as *Deep End*, leaving it to languish in her large bin of cinematic performances.

Dismissing Dors' films

No one was more dismissive of Dors' films than the actress herself, so much so that she even shrugged off her movie career when being celebrated on the TV show *This Is Your Life* in October 1982. Following the presenter's comment that she'd appeared in many films after making *Holiday Camp* in 1947, Dors exclaimed, 'I don't know why!' (Prall 2018: 181). While apparently betraying her heartfelt disappointment about her lack of success in the film industry, this 'off the cuff' remark also implied that the star considered her subsequent thirty-five years of filmmaking to have been a waste of time. It's perhaps not surprising that her biographers subsequently presented Dors' films accordingly, consolidating the idea that her miscellaneous movies had consistently failed to live up to her aspirations and talents, with the single exception of *Yield to the Night*.

Damon Wise, David Bret, Huw Prall and Anna Cale all relegate Dors' film work to something of a professional sideline, enabling the biographers to focus instead on her turbulent personal life (see Wise 1998, Bret 2010, Prall 2018 and Cale 2021). In their accounts, Dors' significant professional achievements include her recording of an album of songs *Swingin' Dors* (Pye Records, 1960), her starring role in the TV sitcom *Queenie's Castle* (1970–72) and her own televised chat show *Open Dors* (1980–81). Consequently, Dors emerges from these publications as a high achieving celebrity who accomplished numerous things in the entertainment business even if she will always be remembered as the British Blonde Bombshell that failed to fulfill her ambition to become a Hollywood movie star. In the star's most recent biography, *The Real Diana Dors*, author Anna Cale describes her subject in a Prologue as a 'talented actress' who 'worked on numerous film and television projects with influential directors, building a fascinating career that spanned decades' (2021: vii). Nevertheless, the biographer's eventual conclusion is markedly different, including the statement that, '[d]espite some great performances, she never seemed to achieve the career trajectory that her acting talent could have garnered' (162–3).

Yet, the attempts of the star and her biographers to write off Dors' film work as a minor activity that contributed little to her fame and fortune should not obscure the fact that there are many reasons why it deserves to be recognised as a significant achievement. Firstly, Dors' cinematic portfolio consists of some very finely crafted productions such as *Oliver Twist* (1948), *Dance Hall* (1950), *A Kid for Two Farthings* (1955) and *Steaming* (1985). Secondly, it comprises some very popular and commercially successful films such as *Here Come the Huggetts* (1948), *An Alligator Named Daisy* (1955), *The Amazing Mr Blunden* (1972), *Theatre of Blood* (1973) and *Adventures of a Taxi Driver* (1975). Thirdly, it features many films of historical and ideological significance, especially in terms of gender and sexuality, hence the attention paid to films such as *The Weak and the Wicked* (1954) and *Passport to Shame* by feminist film scholars (Bell 2010: 114–20 and 142–6). Many more of Dors' movies provide interesting, controversial and challenging depictions of femininity, including *Lady Godiva Rides Again* (1951), *Value for Money* (1955), *The Long Haul* (1957), *I Married a Woman* (1958) and *Keep It*

Up Downstairs. While these have so far received very little attention from feminist film historians, they certainly offer some telling insights into the changing roles of women in postwar cinema and society.

The majority of Dors' films have been written off as trash for too long. Far too many movies have been consigned to the scrapheap of film history after being rubbished by critics, disowned by producers, flopping at the box-office and dropping out of circulation. Yet many of these have the potential to reward consideration, scrutiny and close textual analysis. Moreover, they are no less interesting for being unsuccessful. On the contrary, what makes them fascinating nowadays are those very elements that offended critics and commentators at the time of their original release, unsettling audiences and provoking disapproval. Indeed, several of Dors' biggest critical and commercial disasters contain some of her most intriguing and interesting work, such as *The Unholy Wife*, *Berserk!* (1967) and *The Pied Piper* (1972), as discussed in Chapters 6, 7 and 8. These not only demonstrate that Dors was a highly competent and versatile film actor but also one with the courage to take on contentious and unflattering roles. They even suggest that while she was damned and discarded at the time these films were originally released into cinemas, Dors and her controversial screen anti-heroines provide compelling entertainment for contemporary audiences, especially cult movie fans. In the 21st century, Dors' cinematic work has much more to recommend it than many existing published accounts suggest; a reminder that anything in print should be taken with a pinch of salt.

Some surprising and questionable conclusions

There's no more reason to accept my claims, judgments and observations about Dors than those by the critics and journalists that once dismissed and derided her. My counter-narrative is hardly impartial and can easily be read as a self-professed fan's attempt to restore value to this actress's cinematic performances. Following in Melanie Williams' wake, this book represents another effort to rescue Dors' reputation after years of critical denigration, which stemmed in part from a prejudiced view, one that deems anything associated with femininity, materiality, corporeality and glamour to be intrinsically artificial, superficial and worthless (Williams 2017: 80–81).

I've certainly used this text to celebrate Dors' many achievements within the film industry, partly to salvage a reputation damaged by sustained negative journalistic criticism, public derision and the star's own self-mockery. In addition to highlighting the international aspects of her career, I've also been keen to stress that Dors was a consummate screen performer from a young age, possessing a distinctive and flexible acting style that enabled her to perform effectively across numerous genres over five decades. In doing so, I may well have overplayed my hand now and then, both overestimating the proficiency and power of Dors' big-screen performances and underestimating the contributions and impact of her co-stars, such as Roy Kinnear and Micheal Hordern in *The Pied Piper*, Joan Crawford and Judy Geeson in *Berserk!* and Vanessa Redgrave and Patti Love in *Steaming*.

Maybe something that could have been stressed more throughout my account of Dors' film career is that her status as a movie star was always more apparent than real. There's certainly no doubt that Diana Dors looked like a film star after 1951 and possessed many of the trappings associated with stardom, including the big flashy car and large house with a swimming pool, as well as the furs and jewels. These things may well have persuaded many that she'd attained stardom in the fifties and somehow held on to it thereafter. It's also an irrefutable fact that her high profile celebrity after 1954 earned her star billing on eight separate occasions. Nevertheless, it's also true that most of her time as a film actress was spent performing small supporting roles, often playing characters that seemed insignificant or inconsequential to the main plot. Of those eight star vehicles listed in the opening paragraph of this chapter, Dors only played the central protagonist in *Yield to the Night*, *The Unholy Wife* and *La Ragazza del Palio*. This means that in five of her eight star vehicles she was given intermittent screen time to perform and showcase her attributes and abilities. Meanwhile, a question remains over whether or not she was cast in enough leading roles to warrant the title of 'film star'. In terms of profitability, popularity and output (specifically the number of films produced as vehicles for her), it seems unlikely that Dors was ever quite in the same league as Bette Davis, Margaret Lockwood, Marilyn Monroe and Brigitte Bardot, who all appeared in far more leading roles and generated much greater returns at the box-office.

In economic and institutional terms, a film star's principal function is to guarantee that vast numbers of moviegoers will flock to the cinemas to see a picture on its initial release, stardom being one mechanism used to reduce the inherently unpredictable financial returns of mainstream commercial productions. The ability to guarantee large audiences for a movie is what makes a star a star. This is also what makes a star 'bankable', rendering the actor a relatively safe bet in terms of expenditure. Yet, due to her poor track record at the box-office, Dors couldn't really be considered a major draw. Due to her persistently scandalous tabloid celebrity, her presence in a movie may well have attracted journalistic attention. Yet it's more likely to have generated controversy that could damage the film's commercial prospects than guarantee a profit. Many movie producers no doubt considered Dors to be a bad bet even at the height of her stardom, the majority choosing less controversial and more consistently profitable actors when casting leading roles.

After *Yield to the Night*, *The Unholy Wife* and *La Ragazza del Palio* failed at the box-office between 1956 and 1958, Dors was cast only in supporting parts, often little more than cameos, even when granted top billing. Consequently, the likes of *Passport to Shame*, *Swedish Wildcats* and *Keep It Up Downstairs* were effectively star-billed character roles in which Dors sought to make a big impression with limited screen time by using some of the acting techniques regularly employed by character actors (as discussed in Chapter 8). One of the things I've discovered during the process of working on this book has been just how ambivalent Dors' status as a movie star was throughout her lifetime. Originally believing that she transitioned from being a major star in the fifties to a character actor in the sixties and seventies, I eventually began to perceive how she consistently collapsed the distinction between star and character actor during the early, peak and late stages of her career. Consequently, Dors has proven to be a fascinating case study in terms of film acting since she challenges the idea of star acting as something invariably distinct from character acting.

Analysis of Dors' scenes in several of her star-billed character parts (notably, Frau Poppendick in *The Pied Piper*, Daisy Dureneck in *Keep It Up Downstairs* and Violet in *Steaming*) reveals that she had the advantage of close-ups and spotlights, while often being positioned in the star slot at the epicentre of the screen. This meant that she didn't have to try too hard to gain audience attention. Also, unlike anonymous or little-known actors, Dors brought her distinctive persona and recognisable image to the vast majority of her roles, so that her characters were always quintessentially Dorsian. They almost always possess her wit, charm, laughter, singing and dancing skills, mellifluous voice, as well as her distinctive hairstyle, dagger eyebrows, familiar poses and gestures. In this respect, Dors acted like a star irrespective of the size of her role, as explained in Chapters 5 and 9.

Dors' bright, bold and brazen qualities defined her stardom and made her stand out in a highly competitive industry. Her brains, confidence and indomitable spirit not only enabled her to survive in the film business for almost forty years but also to attract new generations of admirers after her death. Yet these same characteristics made her unpalatable, intimidating and overpowering for many moviegoers, producers, critics and journalists during her lifetime. Without the support of a major film studio, encouragement and approval from critics and a vast army of loyal fans, Dors' film career floundered in the late fifties and sixties (as discussed in Chapters 3 and 4). However, if her failure at this time lay less with her acting talent and more with the negative reaction of studio bosses, critics and mainstream moviegoers, then her cinematic achievements include the way she remained unapologetic and undefeated. Her endurance certainly seems impressive, especially in terms of her posthumous stardom, which has grown steadily since the mid-eighties. What's particularly striking is that, in addition to gaining new fans since 1984, Dors has become an iconic Hollywood-style movie star, even one of the best-known British film actors of the postwar era (see Marchant 2016: 266–74). This is surely what put Dors' image on the cover of Sue Harper's book *Women in British Cinema* in 2000 and Melanie Williams' *Female Stars of British Cinema* in 2016, making her – among other things – the poster girl for British female stardom during the first two decades of the 21st century.

My investigation into the film career of Diana Dors has taught me several other things besides her ambivalent movie star status, her collapsing of star and character acting distinctions and the impressive aspects of her commercial and critical failure. For instance, it's brought home to me that even having all the prerequisites of stardom cannot guarantee success in the film business. With her spectacular looks, repertoire of distinctive mannerisms, acting talent and her propensity to attract intense public interest, Dors had virtually everything she needed to become a major movie star in the 1950s. Even so, her film career was clearly fading fast by the time she reached the age of twenty-five in October 1956. Meanwhile, my exploration of Dors' film work has also indicated that consistent box-office failure and negative critical reviews don't necessarily terminate an actor's film career. Dors' example proves that the ability to stubbornly ignore critical condemnation and derision may indeed result eventually in a cinematic comeback, as it did in her case with the release of *Steaming* a year after her death. It may also lead to a radical reappraisal by subsequent generations of film critics, historians and fans when they begin to see merit in work that was previously overlooked or denigrated for mostly social and ideological reasons rather than artistic ones.

Contemplating Dors' performances across a small but representative body of her cinematic work has also produced some major surprises for me. Chief among them was my eventual realisation that the keynote of her acting was poise – the art of appearing naturally self-confident by remaining physically calm, composed and well-balanced in all situations, especially the most trying. For a star famous for her repertoire of good-time girls, prostitutes, predatory cougars and harridan housewives, it's surprising to find that poise was so central to Dors' performances. The sordid and vulgar qualities of her character types blinded me to that fact that poise consistently added depth and artistry – along with harmony and control – to her work as a film actor. Yet, after comparing her acting in films from across several decades and different genres, it eventually became clear to me that it was poise that provided the foundation upon which Dors constructed some very different kinds of character. Despite the lengths that advocates of the Method went to in the United States in the 1950s to condemn poise as unnatural, insincere and unemotional, Dors clearly retained faith in its power, while proving that it could play a key role in the development of original performances in all kinds of films made in America and Europe from the 1950s to the 1980s, as discussed in Chapters 6 and 9.

Having examined Dors' acting in detail in a selection of five films from across her five-decade career, I remain convinced that her achievements as a film actor were substantial. Not only did she acquire a recognisable set of poses and signature gestures, looks and expressions within a relatively short time but she also capitalised upon her experiences as a model, dancer and Rank Charm School 'scholar' to develop a highly effective acting method by the age of twenty. Close textual analysis has brought home to me that Dors was adept at making subtle adjustments to the scale of her performances, while shifting between naturalistic and histrionic styles according to the type of scene, film and character she was performing, as well as the costumes she was wearing, the audience she was performing to and the performance methods, style and scale of the actors she was playing with, as explained in Chapters 6, 7 and 8. What's just as clear is that Dors made her work for the big screen look almost effortless and very natural. By appearing to act with ease while not taking her work seriously, she added to the impression that little effort and skill was involved in what she did and what she continued doing from the ages of fifteen to fifty-two.

Close attention to Dors' acting in films from the 1940s to the 1980s belies any claim that little thought or effort and skill lay behind these performances. It also contradicts the idea that she and others have expressed, that it was all a waste of time. My experience of watching her movies and scrutinising certain key moments over and over again has been both illuminating and enjoyable. Yet watching a wide assortment of Dors' films has been frustrating at times, particularly when discovering just how few scenes she has despite her star billing. Often this is compensated for by the discovery that her brief appearances provide the film's best moments for me, such as in Dominic Roche's *My Wife's Lodger* (1952) and Danny Kaye's *On the Double* (1961). In films like these, which are best watched with the aid of a fast-forward facility, Dors offers some much-needed respite with succinct performances that are confidently, expertly and deftly executed. It's in such fleeting fragments of film that the actress's skills and spectacular qualities seem to shine most brightly, brevity adding to the intensity of her work, creating something rich and seemingly undiluted. Yet, sadly, even her skills have not been sufficient to make the watching of some films – for example, *It's a Grand Life!* (1953) and *The Sandwich Man* (1965) – worth my while.

These examples prove that Dors was no different to most major movie stars in making her fair share of duds. What seems more unique about her film career is that so much of her best work can be found in commercial disasters and critically derided films such as *The Unholy Wife*, *Berserk!* and *The Pied Piper*, along with others generally dismissed as cheap and inconsequential B-movies, such as *Is Your Honeymoon Really Necessary?*. Just as Dors' appearance in a movie didn't guarantee success at the box-office during the second half of the 20th century, it still doesn't promise a consistently entertaining experience. More often than not, however, her appearance in movies as diverse as *Here Come the Huggetts*, *As Long as They're Happy* (1955), and *Swedish Wildcats* stand out, provoking strong reactions and remaining memorable no matter how brief or incidental.

My Dorsian declarations on the achievements of a remarkably successful failure

Sustaining a five-decade film career in spite of unsuccessful box-office returns, ambivalent journalistic reactions and a barrage of public criticism surely ranks as some kind of achievement. Being given star billing for five movies when playing supporting rather than leading roles seems like another remarkable accomplishment. Having the courage to go on being outspoken, spectacularly blonde and sexy, while continuing to defy conventional moral standards and gender norms deserves respect, at least in my book. Meanwhile, the professionalism, consistency and sheer dogged determination that Dors maintained for so long – particularly in the face of indifference, hostility and scorn – surely has to be deemed impressive by most people. Who could be anything other than impressed by the way that Dors' ended her film career with a fabulous final flourish, starring in one of her most prestigious pictures while succumbing to a terminal illness? Even if my claim that Dors consistently stole the spotlight with captivating and skilful performances in brief film moments seems dubious, then surely all of these other things render the star an outstanding film actor?

But why am I even questioning or doubting these achievements? Taking inspiration from the woman who captivated me as a fifteen-year-old, I'm determined to be bold when presenting my final concluding remarks. Yet it's frustrating to find that – even with my hands placed firmly upon my figurative hips – I can't quite eradicate all trace of equivocation when summarising my findings, which are as follows.

The effort and skill that Dors devoted to film acting between 1946 and 1984 were not wasted. On the contrary, they resulted in a distinctive if not distinguished cinematic oeuvre. For Dors' film portfolio is unique, diverse and full of surprises as well as disappointments. Despite being uneven, it includes many genuinely remarkable performances, sometimes when least expected. Whether these films were commercially successful or critically acclaimed at the time of their original release no longer matters. For the fact is that a significant proportion of them have not only stood the test of time but also come into their own, allowing cult movie aficionados, film buffs and scholars to enjoy and appreciate them, even the gaudiest and goriest of them all.

The nuances of Dors' film performances reveal themselves through close scrutiny and repeated viewings – and certainly with a pause and rewind facility – as well as with an open mind. Both her fleeting film moments and her starring roles repay close and serious attention, making her acting in movies such as *Deep End* and *The Unholy Wife* just as captivating and impressive. As her brief moment in *It's Not Cricket* (1949) demonstrates, Dors certainly didn't need to be billed as the star of a film in order to produce an extraordinary performance. Indeed, it was precisely when cast as an un-named character and given minimal screen time that she responded by raising her game, using all her skills and attributes to seize the spotlight from those billed above her. As a result, she created some of her finest movie moments.

On the other hand, when put into the driving seat of the star vehicles *Yield to the Night*, *The Unholy Wife* and *La Ragazza del Palio,* Dors drew upon a range of things – chiefly versatility, concentration, charisma, patience and stamina – to perform with all kinds of actors in all manner of scenes. Out of some curious and challenging scenarios, she created characters that were credible and compelling despite being conceived of as little more than types; notably, glamour girls, good-time girls, femmes fatales, 'tarts' and harridans. At the same time, she made them uniquely her own by playing them like no one else could do or dared to do. Of course, that's what great movie stars do, especially those that remain watchable, intriguing and pleasurable long after their time is up.

The real stars of cinema transform figments of writers' imaginations into something tangible, engaging and unforgettable. Moreover, they turn their characters into versions of themselves while transforming their own persona into a screen character that audiences can identify with, fall in love with or love to hate. If that's what truly makes a film actor a star, then Diana Dors *was* a movie star. She was indeed the starriest of stars: from her hips to her fingertips; from her luxuriant platinum hair to her toenails; from her dangerous dagger eyebrows to her pouting painted lips. But strip all that away and what's left is an actor of skill, intelligence, range and versatility. Don't let her glitzy image and dismissive comments deceive you. Underneath it all was an actor dedicated to doing her best with whatever she was given and capable of turning a minor movie or even a moment in a minor movie into something momentous. In anyone's book, surely that's no small achievement?

Bibliography

Anonymous (1955), 'Visible Export', *Time* magazine, 10 October, p. 116.
Anonymous (1956), 'Men Don't Dare Look As Diana Comes Out', *New York Post*, 2 July (unpaginated source).
Anonymous (1958), Review of *I Married a Woman*, *Variety*, 7 May (unpaginated source).
Babington, Bruce (ed.) (2001), *British Stars and Stardom: From Alma Taylor to Sean Connery*, Manchester: Manchester University Press.
Baron, Cynthia (2016), *Modern Acting: The Lost Chapter of American Film and Theatre*, London: Palgrave Macmillan.
Baron, Cynthia and Mark Bernard (2013), 'Cult Connoisseurship and American Female Stars in the Sixties: Valuing a Few Withered Tits in the Midst of a Mammary Renaissance', in Kate Egan and Sarah Thomas (eds), *Cult Film Stardom: Offbeat Attractions and Processes of Cultification*, London: Palgrave Macmillan, pp. 259–75.
Basinger, Jeanine (2007), *The Star Machine*, New York: Alfred A. Knopf.
Bell, Melanie (2010), *Femininity in the Frame: Women and 1950s British Popular Cinema*, London and New York: I. B. Tauris.
Bell, Melanie (2016), *Julie Christie*, London: BFI/Palgrave.
Bell, Melanie and Melanie Williams (eds) (2010), *British Women's Cinema*, London and New York: Routledge.
Bolton, Lucy and Julie Lobalzo Wright (eds) (2016), *Lasting Screen Stars: Images that Fade and Personas that Endure*, London: Palgrave.
Bret, David (2010), *Diana Dors: Hurricane in Mink*, London: RJ Books.
Buchwald, Art (1956), 'Britain's Sex Symbol', *New York Herald Tribune*, 2 December (unpaginated source).
Cale, Anna (2021), *The Real Diana Dors*, Barnsley and Philadelphia: Pen & Sword/ White Owl.
Chapman, James, Mark Glancy and Sue Harper (eds) (2007), *The New Film History: Sources, Methods, Approaches*, London: Palgrave.
Chibnall, Steve (2000), *J. Lee Thompson*, Manchester: Manchester University Press.
Cook, Pam (2001), 'The trouble with sex: Diana Dors and the blonde bombshell phenomenon', in Bruce Babington (ed.), *British Stars and Stardom*, Manchester: Manchester University Press, pp. 167–78.

Crist, Judith (1956), 'Diana Dors Happy to be Herself: Denies She's British Marilyn Monroe', *New York Herald Tribune*, 27 June (unpaginated source).
Dors, Diana (1956), 'I'm going to speak my mind', *Picturegoer* ('Out of Dors' column), 31 March, p. 8.
Dors, Diana (1956), 'I can't for ever be a Glamour Bombshell', *Picturegoer* ('Out of Dors' column), 14 April, p. 8.
Dors, Diana (1956), 'Hi Neighbour!', *Picturegoer* ('Out of Dors' column), 26 May, p. 10.
Dors, Diana (1956), 'It's the Gloss That Counts', *Picturegoer* ('Out of Dors' column) 7 July, p. 9.
Dors, Diana (1956), 'What a Fabulous Country', *Picturegoer* ('Out of Dors' column), 14 July, p. 11.
Dors, Diana (1960), *Swingin' Dors*, London: World Distributers Ltd.
Dors, Diana (1981), *Dors by Diana*, London: Queen Anne, Macdonald Futura.
Drake, Philip (2004), 'Jim Carrey: the Cultural Politics of Dumbing Down', in Andy Willis (ed.), *Film Stars: Hollywood and Beyond*, Manchester: Manchester University Press, pp. 71–88.
Duggan, Anne E. (2013), *Queer Enchantments: Gender, Sexuality, and Class in the Fairy-Tale Cinema of Jacques Demy*, Detroit: Wayne State University Press.
Dyer, Richard (1987), *Heavenly Bodies: Film Stars and Society*, London: BFI/Macmillan.
Egan, Kate and Sarah Thomas (eds) (2013), *Cult Film Stardom: Offbeat Attractions and Processes of Cultification*, London: Palgrave Macmillan.
Finnegan, Joe (1960), 'Diana Dors Busy: Hollywood Click Second Time Around', *Newark Evening News*, 18 December (unpaginated source).
Geraghty, Christine (1986), 'Diana Dors', in Charles Barr (ed.), *All Our Yesterdays: 90 Years of British Cinema*, London: BFI, pp. 341–5.
Gledhill, Christine (1991), 'Signs of Melodrama', in Christine Gledhill (ed.) *Stardom: Industry of Desire*, London: Routledge, pp. 207–29.
Graham, Sheila (1956), 'England's Blonde Star Who Resents Being Called Marilyn Monroe', *Sunday Mirror*, 30 September, p. 48.
Hale, Wanda (1957), Review of *Value for Money*, *New York Daily*, 1 August (unpaginated source).
Harper, Sue (2000), *Women in British Cinema: Mad, Bad and Dangerous to Know*, London and New York: Continuum.
Harper, Sue and Justin Smith (2012), *British Film Culture in the 1970s: The Boundaries of Pleasure*, Edinburgh: Edinburgh University Press.
Holt, Paul (1949), 'Looking at the Rushes', in *Picturegoer*, 9 July, p. 5.
Hirsch, Foster (1984), *A Method to their Madness*, New York: Da Capo Press.
Hyams, Joe (1956), 'Sex with Wit', *New York Herald Tribune*, 11 July (unpaginated source).
Johnson, Erskine (1956), 'Diana Competing for Marilyn's Role', *New York World Telegram*, 24 September (unpaginated source).
King, Barry (1991), 'Articulating Stardom', in Christine Gledhill (ed.), *Stardom: Industry of Desire*, London: Routledge, pp. 167–82 [originally published in *Screen*, 26, 5, in September/October 1985].
Krasner, David (2000), 'Strasberg, Adler and Meisner: Method Acting', in Alison Hodge (ed.), *Twentieth Century Actor Training*, London and New York: Routledge, pp. 129–50.

McCullam, William (1956), 'Bombshells on their Travels met with Sighs and Babbles', *New York American*, 5 August (unpaginated source).

McDonald, Paul (2012), 'Story and Show: The Basic Contradiction of Film Star Acting', in Aaron Taylor (ed.), *Theorizing Film Acting*, New York and London: Routledge, pp. 169–83.

Macnab, Geoffrey (1993), *J. Arthur Rank and the British Film Industry*, London: Routledge.

Marchant, Linda (2016), 'Still Famous: Fixing the Star Image of Diana Dors in the Photography of Cornel Lucas', in Lucy Bolton and Julie Lobalzo Wright (eds), *Lasting Screen Stars: Images That Fade and Personas That Endure*, London: Palgrave Macmillan, pp. 261–76.

Mathijs, Ernest (2012), 'From Being to Acting: Performance in Cult Cinema', in Aaron Taylor (ed.), *Theorizing Film Acting*, New York and London: Routledge, pp. 135–51.

Morin, Edgar (2005), *The Stars (Les Stars)*, English translation by Richard Howard, Minneapolis and London: University of Minnesota Press, [originally published in French in 1957].

Murphy, Robert (1989), *Realism and Tinsel: Cinema and Society in Britain 1939–1948*, London: Routledge.

Naremore, James (1988), *Acting in the Cinema*, Berkeley, Los Angeles and London: University of California Press.

Parsons, Louella (1956), 'Diana Dors – Glamor from England', *Pictorial TView*, 26 August, p. 18.

Petley, Julian (2001), 'There's Something about Mary...', in Bruce Babington (ed.), *British Stars and Stardom*, Manchester: Manchester University Press, pp. 205–17.

Prall, Huw (2018), *Passport to Fame: The Diana Dors Story*, Kibworth: Book Guild Publishing.

Sheridan, Simon (2001), *Keeping the British End Up: Four Decades of Saucy Cinema*, London: Titan Books.

Shingler, Martin (2012), *Star Studies: A Critical Guide*, London: BFI/Palgrave.

Smith, Justin (2008), 'Glam, Spam and Uncle Sam: Funding Diversity in 1970s British Film Production', in Robert Shail (ed.), *Seventies British Cinema*, London: BFI/Palgrave Macmillan, pp. 67–80.

Solomon, Matthew (2010), 'Reflexivity and Metaperformance: Marilyn Monroe, Jayne Mansfield and Kim Novak', in R. Barton Palmer (ed.), *Larger Than Life: Movie Stars of the 1950s*, New Brunswick, NJ, and London: Rutgers University Press, pp. 107–29.

Thomas, Bob (1960), 'Diana Dors Tries New Picture Bid', *New York Evening News*, 23 November (unpaginated source).

Thomas, Sarah (2013), '"Marginal moments of spectacle": Character Actors, Cult Stardom and Hollywood Cinema', in Kate Egan and Sarah Thomas (eds), *Cult Film Stardom*, London: Palgrave, pp. 37–54.

Vincendeau, Ginette (2013), *Brigitte Bardot*, London: Palgrave/BFI.

Vineberg, Steve (1991), *Method Actors: Three Generations of an American Acting Style*, New York: Schirmer Books.

Williams, Melanie (2017), *Female Stars of British Cinema: The Women in Question*, Edinburgh: Edinburgh University Press.

Winsten, Archer (1956), untitled source, *New York Post*, 2 July (unpaginated source).
Wood, Thomas (1957), 'Diana Dors: A Perfect Murderess', *New York Herald Tribune*, 3 November (unpaginated source).
Wise, Damon (1998), *Come By Sunday: The Fabulous, Ruined Life of Diana Dors*, Leicester: Charnwood.
Wright Wexman, Virginia (2004), 'Masculinity in Crisis: Method Acting in Hollywood', in Pamela Robertson Wojcik (ed.), *Movie Acting: The Reader*, New York and London: Routledge, pp. 127–44.
Yule, Andrew (1988), *Enigma: David Puttnam, The Story So Far...*, Edinburgh: Mainstream Publishing.

Filmography

Indicating any alternative titles, the name of the director and the date of release, as well as the date of production when significantly different from the release date.

The Shop at Sly Corner, George King, George King Productions, UK 1946.
Holiday Camp, Ken Annakin, Gainsborough Pictures, UK 1947.
Dancing with Crime, John Paddy Carstairs, Coronet Films, UK 1947.
Good-Time Girl, David MacDonald, Rank, UK (made in 1947 but not released until 1950).
Streets Paved with Water, Joe Mendoza, Gainsborough Pictures, UK (made in 1947 but unfinished).
My Sister and I, Harold Huth, Rank, UK 1948.
Penny and the Pownall Case, Slim Hand, Rank, UK 1948.
The Calendar, Arthur Crabtree, Rank, UK 1948.
Oliver Twist, David Lean, Cineguild, UK 1948.
Here Come the Huggetts, Ken Annakin, Rank, UK 1948.
Vote for Huggett!, Ken Annakin, Rank, UK 1949.
It's Not Cricket, Roy Rich and Alfred Roome, Rank, UK 1949.
A Boy, a Girl and a Bike, Ralph Smart, Rank, UK 1949.
Diamond City, David Macdonald, Rank, UK 1950.
Dance Hall, Charles Crichton, Rank, UK 1950.
Worm's Eye View, Jack Raymond, Henry Halstead Productions, UK 1951.
Lady Godiva Rides Again (also known as *Bikini Baby* in USA), Frank Launder, London Films, UK 1951.
The Last Page (aka *Man Bait* in the USA), Terence Fisher, Hammer Films, UK 1952.
My Wife's Lodger, Maurice Elvey, David Dent Productions, UK 1952.
The Great Game, Maurice Elvey, David Dent Productions, UK 1953.
The Saint's Return (aka *The Saint's Girl Friday*), Seymour Friedman, Hammer Films, UK 1953.
Is Your Honeymoon Really Necessary?, Maurice Elvey, David Dent Productions, UK 1953.

It's a Grand life!, John Blakeley, Mancunian Films, UK 1953.
The Weak and the Wicked, J. Lee Thompson, Marble Arch Productions, UK 1954.
As Long as They're Happy, J. Lee Thompson, Group Films, UK 1955.
Miss Tulip Stays the Night, Leslie Arliss, Jaywell Films, UK 1955.
A Kid for Two Farthings, Carol Reed, London Films, UK 1955.
Value for Money, Ken Annakin, Group Films, UK 1955.
An Alligator Named Daisy, J. Lee Thompson, Rank, UK 1955.
Yield to the Night (aka as *Blonde Sinner* in the USA), J. Lee Thompson, Kenwood Productions, UK 1956.
I Married a Woman, Hal Kanter, Gomalco Productions, USA (made in 1956, released in 1958).
The Unholy Wife, John Farrow, RKO/John Farrow Productions, USA 1957.
The Long Haul, Ken Hughes, Marksman Productions, UK 1957.
La Ragazza del Palio/The Girl of the Palio (aka as *The Love Specialist*), Luigi Zampa, Cité Films, Italy/France 1958.
Tread Softly Stranger, Gordon Parry, George Minter Productions, UK 1958.
Passport to Shame (aka *Room 43*), Alvin Rakoff, United Co-Productions, UK 1959.
Scent of Mystery (aka *Holiday in Spain*), Jack Cardiff, Mike Todd Jr. Productions, USA 1960.
On the Double, Melville Shavelson, Dena Productions, USA 1961.
King of the Roaring '20s, Joseph M. Newman, Bischoff-Diamond Productions, USA 1961.
Mrs Gibbons Boys, Max Varnel, Halstead Productions, UK 1962.
West 11, Michael Winner, Angel Productions, UK 1963.
Allez France! (aka *The Counterfeit Constable*), Robert Dhéry, CICC Productions, France 1964.
The Sandwich Man, Robert Hartford-Davis, Titan International, UK 1965.
Berserk! (aka *Circus of Blood*), Jim O'Connelly, Herman Cohen Productions, UK 1967.
Danger Route, Seth Holt, Amicus Productions, UK 1967.
Hammerhead, David Miller, Irving Allen Productions, UK 1968.
Baby Love, Alastair Reed, Avton Films, UK 1968.
There's a Girl in My Soup, Roy Boulting, Charter Film Productions, UK 1970.
Deep End, Jerzy Skolimowski, Bavaria Atelier Films, UK/West Germany 1970.
Hannie Calder, Burt Kennedy, Cutwel Productions, UK 1971.
The Pied Piper, Jacques Demy, Sagittarius Productions, UK/West Germany/USA 1972.
Swedish Wildcats (aka *Every Afternoon*), Joe Sarno, Unicorn Enterprises, UK 1972.
The Amazing Mr Blunden, Lionel Jeffries, Helmdale Films, UK 1972.
Steptoe & Son Ride Again, Peter Sykes, Associated London Films, UK 1973.
Theatre of Blood, Douglas Hickox, Cinema Productions, UK 1973.
Nothing but the Night, Peter Sasdy, Charlemagne Productions, UK 1973.
From Beyond the Grave, Kevin Connor, Amicus Productions, UK 1974.
The Infernal Doll (aka *Craze*), Freddie Francis, Harbour Productions, UK 1974.
The Amorous Milkman, Derren Nesbit, Twickenham Films, UK 1975.
What the Swedish Butler Saw, Vernon Becker, Films AB Robur, Sweden/USA 1975.

Bedtime with Rosie, Wolf Rilla, London International Films, UK 1975.
Three for All, Martin Campbell, Dejanus Films, UK 1975.
Adventures of a Taxi Driver, Stanley Long, Salon Productions, UK 1975
Keep It Up Downstairs, Robert Young, Pyramid Pictures, UK 1976.
Adventures of a Private Eye, Stanley Long, Salon Productions, UK 1977
Confessions from the David Galaxy Affair, Willy Roe, Roldvale Productions, UK 1979.
Steaming, Joseph Losey, Worldfilm Series, UK 1985.

Index

acting, 29–30, 92, 94–6, 98, 102, 105, 108, 110, 112–14, 116–17, 122–4, 126–7, 131, 133–4, 140–2, 147–50
   awards, 31, 32, 38, 45, 130
   British school, 103, 108
   cameo, 34, 125–6, 139, 146
   character acting, 5, 24, 94–6, 123–4, 126–7, 131, 133–4, 146
   cult, 112–13
   ham, 127
   has-been, 116
   histrionic, 113, 122–3, 148
   improvisation, 99, 100, 102, 140–1
   melodramatic, 133
   Method, 42–3, 99, 100–8, 141, 148
   naturalistic, 18, 30, 79, 89, 96, 97, 125, 129, 133–4, 138, 148
   over-acting, 95–6, 102, 115, 125, 127
   pantomimic, 122
   pseudo-star acting, 98
   referential, 114, 116
   scene stealing, 96
   star acting, 91–92, 94–5, 98, 116
   star-character acting, 126–7
   virtuosic, 118, 127
   vivid expressiveness, 5, 96, 123, 124, 131
Actors Studio in New York City, 19, 42, 101, 104
Adair, Hazel, 81–2
Adler, Stella, 103, 104, 141
Adventures of a Private Eye, 83
Adventures of a Taxi Driver, 81, 143
ageing, 68, 70, 81, 84, 109
All Our Saturdays (TV sitcom), 80
Allez France!, 126
Alligator Named Daisy, An, 43, 45, 47, 126, 143
Amazing Mr Blunden, The, 80, 143

Amorous Milkman, The, 81
Annakin, Ken, 13
As Long as They're Happy, 43–4, 49, 149
Asher, Jane, 139
Attenborough, Richard, 16, 29
audacious, 141
autobiography, 23, 68, 78, 83–5, 109
awards, 31, 32, 38, 45, 130

B Movies, 19, 43, 60–1, 74, 89, 149
Babington, Bruce, 6, 13
Baby Love, 79
BAFTA (British Academy of Film and Television), 38, 45, 128, 139
Baker, George, 75–6
Bardot, Brigitte, 33, 73–4, 145
Baron, Cynthia, 103
basque, 44, 69, 113, 123; *see also* corset
Beatles, The, 1, 2
beauty, 22, 47, 85, 89
beauty parades, pageants and contests, 15, 34
Becker, Vernon, 80–1
Behind Closed Dors (autobiography), 83
Bedtime with Rosie, 81
Bell, Melanie, 6, 32, 41
Bentine, Michael, 79
Berserk!, 79, 83, 109–17, 122, 144, 145, 149
Best, George, 140
bikini, 32–5, 46, 64
Bikini Baby (aka *Lady Godiva Rides Again*), 35, 47
Billy Smart's Circus, 112
bit-parts, 18, 38, 73
Black Narcissus, 16
Blackman, Honor, 19, 21, 25–6
Blake, Peter, 1
bleached hair, 33, 37, 69

blonde bombshell, 36, 40, 42, 46, 49, 52, 57–8, 63, 69, 70, 74, 79, 100, 143
Bondi, Beulah, 62
Born Yesterday (play), 31, 36
bosom, 44, 97, 113; *see also* breasts
Box, Betty, 20
Box, Muriel, 20–1
Box, Sydney, 16, 20–1
Boy, a Girl and a Bike, A, 25–6
Brando, Marlon, 1, 42, 44, 56
brazen, 44, 120, 146
breasts, 26, 32, 39, 44, 58, 69, 70, 130; *see also* bosom
Brent, George, 35
Bret, David, 37, 143
British New Wave, 27
British school of acting, 103, 108
Britishness, 69
Bruce, Brenda, 129, 136
Bryan, Dora, 27, 34
Buchanan, Jack, 43–4

Cadillac sports car, 72, 78
Cale, Anna, 143
cameo roles and acting, 34, 125–6, 139, 146
cancer, 132
Cannes film festival, 7, 32, 45, 73, 128
Carpenter, Joan (hair stylist), 132
celebrity, 32, 34, 77, 118, 125, 126, 143, 145, 146
character acting, 5, 24, 94–6, 123–4, 126–7, 131, 133–4, 146
characterisation, 92–3, 108, 125–6, 131, 151
charisma, 47, 146, 151
Chibnall, Steve, 33
Christie, Julie, 78–9
Churchill, Winston, 54
Cinematograph Act 1948, 20
Clark, Petula, 22, 27, 29
cleavage, 3, 91, 120
Cohen, Herman, 109–10, 117
confidence, 40, 51–2, 57, 77, 83, 86, 89, 98, 127, 135, 146, 148
controversy, 65, 138, 146
Cook, Pam, 6, 7
Collins, Joan, 19, 34
Colleano, Bonar, 27, 89, 96
Columbia Pictures, 110, 119, 130
Confessions from the David Galaxy Affair, 83, 142
corporeal, 141, 144
corset, 26, 40, 44, 69–70, 123, 141; *see also* basque
costume, 26, 29, 43, 45, 46, 48, 49, 55–6, 58, 65–67, 69–71, 75, 79, 113, 120–3, 130, 137, 148
Crawford, Joan, 69, 79, 109, 113, 116, 145

Craze (aka *The Infernal Doll*), 80
Crichton, Charles, 27, 29
Crist, Judith, 57
cult audiences and fans, 112, 117, 144, 150
cult movies, 112–14, 116, 144
Cushing, Peter, 80

dance, 23, 26, 27, 29, 146
Dance Hall, 8, 27–8, 29, 34, 48, 143
Danger Route, 79
Davis, Bette, 38, 55, 145
Dawson, Richard (Dickie), 77
De Banzie, Brenda, 44, 75
Dean, Felicity, 129
Dean, James, 43, 56, 104
Decker, Diana, 89
Deep End, 139–42, 150
Demy, Jacques, 118–19, 127
Denham Studios, 19
Dent, David, 35, 93
deportment, 19, 30, 134
Diamond City, 25, 29
Dickens, Charles, 16
Dodds, Olive, 19
Donovan (Phillips Leitch), 119, 126
Dors by Diana (autobiography), 23, 68, 84–5, 102, 109
Dorsian (poses and attitudes typical of Diana Dors), 100, 113, 120, 134, 146
Duggan, Anne, 119.
dumb blonde stereotype, 38, 42
Dunn, Nell, 85, 128, 130
Dyer, Richard, 39–40

Ealing Films, 18, 19, 27, 29
earnings, 37, 45, 51, 109; *see also* salary
Eighties (1980s), 84
Ekberg, Anita, 32, 65
elocution, 15, 19, 134
Elvey, Maurice, 35, 89, 93
Ewell, Tom, 38, 40
exploitation thrillers, 110, 112–13, 117
eye-catching, 56–7, 71, 123; *see also* spectacular appearance
eyebrows, 52–3, 98, 131, 146, 151
eyelashes, 23, 24, 29, 52, 76, 77, 113, 114, 120, 131

fading stars and stardom, 110
farce, 36, 82
Farrar, David, 26, 29
Farrow, John, 100
femininity, 39, 41, 52, 54–5, 73, 78, 86, 91, 143, 144
feminism, 84–5, 128–30, 143

femme fatale, 63, 75, 77, 101, 115, 151
Fifties (1950s), 37–42
film audiences, 112, 148, 151
fingers, 105–6, 115, 151
Fisher, Terence, 35
For Adults Only (autobiography), 83–4, 142
forthrightness, 54, 56, 65
Forties (1940s), 14
From Beyond the Grave, 80

Gainsborough Pictures, 16, 18, 19, 20, 29, 35
Gassman, Vittorio, 71–2
Gaumont-British, 18
gay men, 56, 68, 85
Gender, 41, 91, 150
Gentlemen Prefer Blondes, 37–8, 46
Geraghty, Christine, 6, 7, 32
Geeson, Judy, 79, 112–13, 145
Germain, Larry (Makeup Artist), 65
Gilliat, Sidney, 31, 34, 84
Girl Can't Help It, The, 60
glamour, 14, 15, 21, 23, 35, 36, 39, 42, 45, 65, 67, 74, 86, 110, 111, 129, 130, 132, 137, 138, 144
Glamour Girl type, 14–16, 24, 29, 35, 36, 49, 67, 70, 74, 76, 93, 151
Gobel, George, 51, 61, 66
Good-Time Girl, 14, 16, 20–21, 48
gossip columnists, 59–60
Gough, Michael, 112
Graham, Sheila, 60
Grant, Cary, 134, 135
Great Game, The, 33, 36, 44, 96
Gregson, John, 45–6
Griffith, Kenneth, 15
Grimm Brothers, 118–19
grotesque, 125, 141
guest star roles, 43, 118, 123–6
Guinness, Alec, 17
Gynt, Greta, 14, 41

hairstyles, 2, 23, 32, 34, 35, 40, 50, 52, 70, 79, 123, 131–2, 137, 146, 151
Hale, Wanda, 46
ham actors, 127
Hamilton, Dennis, 35, 36, 40, 51
Hammer Films, 31
Hammerhead, 79
hands-on-hips pose, 29, 97, 100, 101, 113, 114–15, 120, 135, 136
Harbord, Gordon, 16
Hardin, Ty, 110–13, 115–16
Harper, Sue, 32, 147
harridans, 79–80, 148, 151
Harris, Julie (costume designer), 45

Harrison, Cathryn, 122
Harrison, Evangeline (costume designer), 121, 123
Harrison, Kathleen, 16, 17, 22
has-beens, 109, 110, 112, 116
Haworth, Jann, 1
Henshaw, Gladys, 34
Here Come the Huggetts, 8, 13, 14, 22, 23, 143, 149
Hickson, Joan, 45
hips, 24, 29, 151
Hird, Thora, 36
Hirsch, Foster, 103, 104
histrionic acting, 113, 122–3, 148; *see also* theatricality
Hitchcock, Alfred, 114, 126, 134
Holiday Camp, 13, 22, 29, 142
Holloway, Stanley, 34, 45
Hollywood ambitions, 35, 50, 51, 65, 143
Hollywood star machine, 37, 42
Holt, Paul, 24, 49
Holt, Seth, 27
Homolka, Oscar, 15, 29
Hordern, Michael, 145
horror movies, 80, 110, 128, 142
How to Marry a Millionaire, 37, 46
Howarth, Donald, 80
Hughes, Ken, 74, 78
humiliation, 77, 109
Hurt, John, 120–2
husbands
    Dawson, Richard (Dickie), 77
    Hamilton, Dennis, 35, 36, 40, 51
    Lake, Alan, 80
Hyams, Joe, 52–9

I Married a Woman, 9, 51, 60–4, 66, 71, 143
idiolect, 92, 99, 101–2; *see also* mannerisms and trademark gestures
impersonation, 94–5
improvisation, 99, 100, 102, 140–1
Infernal Doll, The (aka *Craze*), 80
inflatable sex doll, 54, 75; *see also* sex doll
international appeal, stardom, success and fame, 47, 50, 145
intimacy, 48
irony, 76, 112
Is Your Honeymoon Really Necessary?, 7, 9, 36–7, 89–98, 99, 133–4, 149
It's a Grand life!, 37, 149
It's Not Cricket, 2–5, 22, 96, 126, 150
Italy, 71–3

Jackson, Glenda, 8, 69, 128
James, Sidney (aka Sid), 34, 90, 97

jitterbug (dance), 16, 36
Johnson, Celia, 45
Johnson, Richard, 79

Kaye, Danny, 78, 149
Kazan, Elia, 43, 104–5
Keep It Up Downstairs, 81–3, 138, 143, 146
Kendall, Kay, 34
Kent, Jean, 14, 20–21
Kid for Two Farthings, A, 31, 32, 43, 45, 143
King, Barry, 10, 94
King, George, 13
King of the Roaring '20s, 78
Kinnear, Roy, 145
Krasner, David, 107

Lady Godiva Rides Again (aka *Bikini Baby*), 31–4, 84, 126, 143
Lake, Alan, 80
LAMDA (London Academy of Music and Dramatic Art), 15
The Last Page (aka *Man Bait*), 33, 35
laugh and laughter, 53, 136, 146
Launder, Frank, 31, 34, 84
Lean, David, 17, 20, 29, 45, 79
Lee, Belinda, 19, 49
Lee, Christopher, 19
Lee Thompson, J., 48, 142
legs, 15, 23, 26, 29, 44, 67, 113, 115
Lime Grove Studios, 19
lips, 47, 114, 115, 131, 134, 135
Lisette (play), 27
Lockwood, Margaret, 13, 14, 19, 145
Lollabrigida, Gina, 47
Lom, Herbert, 20, 75
Long Haul, The, 74–7, 143
Longhurst, Sue, 81, 83
Los Angeles, 50, 64, 68, 77–8, 109
Losey, Joseph, 85, 128–9
Love, Patti, 129–31, 136, 145

McCallum, John, 26, 29, 34
McDonald, Paul, 10, 94
Macnab, Geoffrey, 19
Madoc, Philip, 111, 113
Malenotti, Maleno, 71
Man Bait (aka *The Last Page*), 35, 47
Man of the World (play), 31
mannerisms, 25, 38, 96, 147; *see also* idiolect and trademark gestures
Mansfield, Jayne, 32, 56, 60, 68
Maret Jr, Harry (hair stylist), 65
masculinity, 54, 63–4, 91
Mathijs, Ernest, 10, 95–6, 112, 114, 116, 123, 125–6

Mature, Victor, 74–7
measurements, 57, 59; *see also* vital statistics
Meisner, Sanford, 102, 107, 108, 141
melodrama, 62, 108, 133
Method acting, 42–3, 99, 100–8, 141, 148
Metro-Goldwyn-Mayer (MGM), 18, 43
Mildred Pierce, 112, 117
Miles, Sarah, 129, 130
Miller, Jonathan, 85
Millington, Mary, 81, 82
mink bikini, coat and/or stole, 32, 66, 69
Miranda (play), 31, 36
Miss Tulip Stays the Night, 31, 43, 138
Mitchell, Yvonne, 41, 48
Mitchum, Robert, 38, 74
modelling, 15, 29, 134, 148
Monroe, Marilyn, 1, 8, 9, 32–3, 37–42, 44, 46, 46, 49, 51–3, 56–60, 64–5, 68, 73–4, 104, 145
Morgan, Terence, 75
Morin, Edgar, 23, 25
Moulder-Brown, John, 139–40
My Wife's Lodger, 31, 36–37, 149

Naremore, James, 134, 135
National Enquirer, 59
naturalistic acting, 18, 30, 79, 89, 96–7, 125, 129, 133–4, 138, 148
Neighborhood Playhouse, 102, 107–8
Nettheim, David, 126–7
New York City, 51, 64
New York Daily News, 46
New York Herald Tribune, 52, 57–8, 66
New York Mirror, 52
New York Post, 52
Newley, Anthony, 17, 29
Nothing but the Night, 80
Novak, Kim, 56

O'Connelly, Jim, 117
Oedipus Tyrannus (play), 85
Oliver Twist (film), 8, 14, 17, 20, 29, 96, 143
Oliver Twist (novel), 17
Olivier, Laurence, 51, 60
On the Double, 78, 149
On the Waterfront, 43, 100, 104–5
Open Dors (TV chat show), 143
Ouspenskaya, Maria, 103–4
over-acting, 95–6, 102, 115, 125, 127

pantomime, 122–4
Paramount Pictures, 18
parody, 82
Parsons, Louella, 59
Passport to Shame, 6, 74–5, 138, 143, 146

pastiche, 117
Penny and the Pownall Case, 20
performance, 29–30, 48, 92, 94–6, 98, 102, 105, 108, 110, 112–13, 114, 116–17, 122–4, 126–7, 129, 131, 133, 134, 138, 140, 142, 144, 147–50
personification, 94–5
Petley, Julian, 82
Pettingell, Frank, 36, 45–6
Picturegoer, 24, 48–9, 58
Pied Piper, The, 7, 80, 118–27, 144–6, 149
Pinewood Studios, 19, 51
pin-up, 23, 29, 37, 39
Pleasence, Donald, 45
poise, 98, 105, 108, 129, 134–5, 138, 148
pornography, 80
pouting lips, 15, 29, 57–58, 101, 115, 120, 151
Prall, Huw, 143
Price, Dennis, 20, 34
Price, Vincent, 80
prostitutes and prostitution, 75, 81, 103, 120, 148
pseudo-star performance, 98
publicity, 32, 35, 36, 47, 55, 70, 110
Puttnam, David, 119, 124

Queenie's Castle (TV sitcom), 80, 143
'Quota Quickies', 20

Radford, Basil, 2–5, 22
Ragazza del Palio, La/The girl of the Palio (aka *The Love Specialist*), 9, 71–2, 138, 145
Rank, J. Arthur, 14
Rank Charm School, 13, 19, 148
Rank Organisation, 13, 14, 16, 18–22, 25–6, 28, 31, 42, 43, 45, 46–7, 50
Rapper, Irving, 60
Rebel Without a Cause, 43, 56
Redgrave, Vanessa, 85, 129, 130, 145
Reed, Carol, 31, 45
referential acting, 114, 116
RKO (Radio-Keith-Orpheum), 9, 50, 51, 59, 64–5, 67, 71, 108
Robson, Flora, 20–1, 29
romantic comedy, 45, 56, 57, 67, 71–2
Rossellini, Renzo, 71
Royal Court Theatre, 80, 124
Rushton, Willy, 82
Rutherford, Margaret, 45, 126

Sagoe, Sally, 129
Saint's Return, The, 31, 126
salary, 16, 51; *see also* earnings
Sandwich Man, The, 79, 126, 149
Sarno, Joe, 80
Sassy, 3, 23, 37, 39, 42, 63; see also smart

scene stealing, 96
self-mockery, 46, 54, 69, 117, 145
self-possession, 40, 71, 75
Sellers, Peter, 80
Sgt. Pepper's Lonely Hearts Club Band, 1
Seven Year Itch, The, 38, 40, 42, 58, 60, 64
Seventies (1970s), 70, 80, 82
sex comedies, 80–4, 128, 142
sex doll, 54, 75; *see also* inflatable sex doll
sex symbol(s), 5–6, 39, 41, 57, 59, 68–9, 73, 79, 81, 84, 109, 115, 117
sexual abuse, 20, 84, 132, 141
sexuality, 41, 69
Shakespeare, William, 85
Shand Gibbs, Sheila, 36
Shaw, Susan, 14, 19, 21, 22, 25
Shop at Sly Corner, The, 13, 14, 15, 22, 29, 96, 136
shoulderless gowns, 36, 44, 49, 69, 72
Shoup, Howard (costume designer), 65–6
Sim, Alastair, 34, 126
Simmons, Jean, 16, 54
Sindon, Donald, 19, 45
Sixties (1960s), 69, 78
Skolimowski, Jerzy, 139
Slocombe, Douglas, 27
smart, 42, 53, 57, 64, 71, 72; *see also* sassy
soft-core sex films, 80–1, 84, 142
spectacular appearance, 65, 89, 96, 97, 113, 124, 130, 137, 147, 149; *see also* eye-catching
Spiderwoman persona, 106, 108, 115
Stanislavsky, Konstantin, 103
Stanwyck, Barbara, 38, 65, 76
star acting, 91–92, 94–5, 98, 116
star-character acting, 126–7
star image, 40–41, 51, 72, 92–3, 96, 125, 129, 134, 135, 146
star slot, 5, 44, 96, 97, 123, 146
star vehicles, 38, 48–50, 55, 71–2, 89, 145, 151
starlet, 14, 20–2, 23, 25, 29, 31, 43, 46, 50, 54, 133
Strasberg, Lee, 19, 42, 103, 104, 105, 141
Steaming (film), 7, 9, 128–37, 143, 145, 146, 147
Steaming (play), 128
Steiger, Rod, 51, 62, 64, 79, 100–2, 104, 105
Stephen, Susan, 45
Steptoe & Son Ride Again, 80
Swedish Wildcats, 80, 138, 142, 146, 149
Swingin' Dors (autobiography), 15, 78
Swingin' Dors (LP), 78, 143
swinging-hip walk, 58, 115; *see also* wiggle walk

'tart', 18, 74, 83, 135, 151
taste and tastelessness, 56, 70

Taurog, Norman, 61
Theatre, 31, 42, 85, 94, 124
Theatre of Blood, 80, 143
theatricality, 113–14, 121, 125, 127, 131; *see also* histrionic acting
There's a Girl in My Soup, 80
Thesiger, Ernest, 45–6
This Is Your Life (TV show), 142
Thomas, Sarah, 10, 96
Three for All, 81
Three Months Gone (play), 80, 124, 139
Time magazine, 47
Timon of Athens (TV adaptation of William Shakespeare's play), 85
Tomlinson, David, 90, 93
trademark gestures, 25, 97, 99, 127, 129, 146, 148; *see also* idiolect and mannerisms
   hands-on-hips pose, 29, 97, 100, 101, 113, 114–15, 120, 135, 136
   pouting lips, 15, 29, 57–58, 101, 115, 120, 151
   swinging-hip walk, 58, 115; *see also* wiggle walk
transnational stardom, 69
Tread Softly Stranger, 74–7, 83, 138
Tryon, Tom, 62, 102, 105–8, 115–16, 141
Tushingham, Rita, 78
Twentieth Century-Fox, 18, 37, 42
21 Club, 51, 53, 64
Turner, Lana, 33, 37, 45
Two Ronnies, The, 85; *see also The Worm That Turned*
typecasting, 95

Unholy Wife, The, 7, 9, 51, 62, 64–7, 77, 99–108, 115–16, 138, 141, 144, 145, 146, 148, 150–1
Universal Pictures, 64
Upstairs, Downstairs (TV series), 81–2

Vadim, Roger, 73
Value for Money, 33, 43, 45, 143
vamp and vamping, 22, 24
Variety, 46, 66
Vaughan, Peter, 121
Venice film festival, 7, 32, 43, 139
versatility, 74, 100, 108, 144–5, 151
Versois, Odile, 75
Vincendeau, Ginette, 73
Vineberg, Steve, 101
virtuosic acting, 118, 127
vital statistics, 57, 59; *see also* measurements
vivid expressiveness, 5, 96, 123, 124, 131
voice, 54, 76, 91, 95, 96, 100, 101–2, 107, 115, 122, 134, 135, 140, 146
Vote for Huggett!, 22, 25
vulnerability, 39–40, 76, 133

Walsh, Kay, 17
Warner, Jack, 16, 22, 27, 29
Warner Bros., 18
Wayne, John, 63
Wayne, Naunton, 2–5, 22
Weak and the Wicked, The, 6, 32, 48, 143
weight loss and gain, 33–35, 70, 84
West, Mae, 1, 24, 37, 82
What the Swedish Butler Saw, 80, 142
wiggle walk, 58, 115; *see also* swinging-hip walk
Wild, Jack, 83, 126
Wilde, Oscar, 1, 78
Wilder, Billy, 38, 58
Williams, Melanie, 8, 32, 144, 147
Winmill, Sammie, 126–7
Winsten, Archer, 52–4
Wise, Damon, 20, 52, 143
wit, 52–3, 76, 86, 102, 146
working men's clubs, 84, 109
Worm That Turned, The (comedy serial on *The Two Ronnies*), 85
Wright Wexman, Virginia, 103

Yield to the Night, 6, 8, 31, 32, 33, 48–9, 51, 60, 84, 100, 138, 143, 145–6, 151

Zampa, Luigi, 71